Symposium on Creation·II

Symposium on Creation II

by

Donald W. Patten and Others

BAKER BOOK HOUSE
Grand Rapids, Michigan

ISBN: 0-8010-6896-7

Library of Congress Catalog Card Number: 68-19213

First Printing, February 1970
Second Printing, August 1971

FOREWORD

Centuries ago the church ruled the western world, doing such a poor job of it that the resulting span of time is almost universally called the "Dark Ages." Christ, however, did not give the church the job of ruling; the church was given the job of teaching and witnessing.

With the coming of Biblical publishing in native languages of Europe came the Reformers, and following them came a new understanding of the Bible, of God, of man, of superior economic relationships, superior governmental structures, and of purpose of life. This new complex of values and principles is frequently called the "Protestant Ethic," an ethic grounded on the Scriptures. It prepared the way for the development of the greatest civilization and technology in the history of man.

But today western civilization is staggering. The Protestant Ethic is deeply eroding in the wake of western affluence, or wealth. Former virtues are no longer classed as virtues, and likewise, former vices are no longer classed as vices. Biblically-oriented morality is being progressively challenged and replaced by offshoots of atheism such as anarchism, Bolshevism, collectivism, Fabianism, and the like. And atheism finds its excuse for existence — and some say its virility — in Darwinism — evolution — evolutionary uniformitarianism — call it what one may.

We perceive that evolutionary uniformitarianism is not science. It may be mythology. It may be a philosophy. But especially, it may be a psychological crutch. By way of illustration, when Adam and Eve elected or preferred to flee from both the knowledge of God and the presence of God, they felt a need of a crutch or some sort of cover-up, in that case, fig leaves.

And so it is, we suspect, with several recent generations of affluent western intellectuals, men who have also frequently elected to flee from the knowledge and the moral presence of the Creator. A scientific cover-up was apparently required here also. And so, in the process of time, a sewed-up patchwork of supposedly scientific cloth was manufactured, and was widely distributed. The system was generated by the cynicism inherent in German rationalism. It was structured around Kant's nebular hypothesis in astronomy. It was braided around Hutton's and Lyell's uniformitarian myth in historical geology. And it was completed with the leaves of Darwin's evolutionary network.

We maintain that this patchwork of thought is neither necessary nor scientific. (Nor is it adequate history.) Declaring this, with strong evidence, bares open the very soul of western civilization, an agonizing condition for some, and, no doubt, a welcome condition to others.

This is the second of a projected series of Symposiums on Creation. In this volume, and even more so in the total series, a program of balances is intended to be achieved. These are:

1. A balance between biological subject materials and earth history (geophysical materials).
2. A balance between catastrophism and creationism, forming a dual framework of thought.
3. A balance between negative assertions (identifying mistaken ideas) with positive conclusions, ideas and proposals, constructive in nature.
4. A balance between the philosophical and the scientific. (Within the philosophical we include the theological; within the scientific we include the historical.)
5. A balance between practical and theoretical thought.
6. A balance between recognized and defensible assumption, and logical conclusion.

We object to the evolutionary mythology as if it were a shelter for the atheism to which it frequently leads, and for which it is used as defense. We object to the evolutionary mythology inasmuch as it is part and parcel of a modern, neo-pagan, western syndrome. Yet this objection is the lesser of two goals.

More importantly, an understanding of earth history within the framework of catastrophism and creation opens up the panorama of creation in its grandeur, in its majesty, in its magnificence, in its precision, and this presents a perhaps dim, but glorious reflection of the majesty of God our Creator and sovereign. This in turn provides us with a better insight, and a more realistic approach to the more mundane subject of man with his twentieth century set of problems and new code of ethics, with its concomitant violence — man with his fig leaves, his inability to stand prosperity, his pride, his deep and profound spiritual needs, which Christ met in His redemption and in His teachings.

Here, men of faith and experience in science grapple with age-old questions, unshackled by the bonds of evolutionary uniformitarianism. Here thoughtful essays will grip your interest, and will add insight into specific problems. And perhaps here one may find the rosy fingers of a happier dawn, when men of deep faith and great learning unfold some of the secrets God has placed in His universe for the benefit of mankind, all of which in turn reflect the glory of God.

Donald W. Patten, Editor

TABLE OF CONTENTS

The Pre-flood Greenhouse Effect

(The Antediluvian Canopy)

Donald W. Patten

DONALD W. PATTEN

Donald W. Patten may be called both a businessman and a scholar. A Montanan by birth and a geographer by training and lifelong interest, he began reading the Bible while in college, taking courses including evolution. As a student in college, he experienced conversion to the Christian faith. Shortly thereafter, he was given pulpit duties in a small, rural, community church in the village of Lolo, Montana.

He received a B.A. in geography from the University of Washington in 1951, and a M.A., also in geography, in 1962. He is the owner of a microfilming business in Seattle, and is also the founder of the Pacific Meridian Publishing Company.

His publications include *The Biblical Flood and the Ice Epoch*, a book making synthetical investigation into the nature of the Flood catastrophe from the geographical perspective. He is also the editor of both *Symposium on Creation* (I) and now this current endeavor, *Symposium on Creation II*.

THE PRE-FLOOD GREENHOUSE EFFECT
(The Antediluvian Canopy)

What was the atmosphere of the earth like, and what was the climate of the earth like in the era before the flood? There is evidence that climates have changed dramatically, permanently and suddenly. In Arctic regions there is evidence of former luxuriant sub-tropical forests, and even huge fossil palm leaves within 800 miles of the North Pole. About 200 miles from the South Pole, where temperatures are so cold that today life cannot flourish, Admiral Byrd found fossil evidence of a once luxuriant forest.

Or in the remote cold reaches of the Northern Hemisphere, on the island of Spitzbergen, north of northern Norway, it is sufficiently cold today that ice breakers have trouble approaching even during the few weeks of late summer. Here on Spitzbergen (Svalbard in Norwegian) fossils of marine crustaceans are found which could only have lived in tropical waters. We suspect that not only have climates changed with drama, permanence and suddenness, but so also have ocean temperatures changed remarkably, if not quite so suddenly.

We have ample indication that many of the animals which lived in the pre-flood, primordial period were large — generally much larger than present animal counterparts. There were lizards, for instance, which weighed 40 tons (the brontosaurus dinosaur). There were sloths which weighed 10,000 pounds. There were insects such as butterflies with 20-inch wing spans. (What must mosquitoes have been like in this primordial era?)

Again, there were some birds with 25- and 30-foot wing spans, which laid eggs 11 inches in diameter — two gallon eggs. Recently a condor with an 18-foot wing span was unearthed, again suggesting an era in which relatively large animals were common, and gigantism among animals was normal. Interestingly enough, fossil impressions of human footprints, some measuring 20 and 22 inches from toe to heel have also been unearthed.[1,2] The Scriptures,

---

[1]Smith, A. E. Wilder, *Man's Origin, Man's Destiny*, Wheaton, Ill., Harold Smith Publishers, 1968, pp. 96-97, 136-137. Items are credited to geologist Clifford L. Burdick.

[2]These fossil human footprint impressions are side by side with dinosaur

too, suggest that "there were giants in the earth in those days" (Genesis 6:4).

There are traditions from many ancient sources which suggest that man lived longer in a former era. Genesis teaches us that man lived about nine centuries, a far cry from the current threescore and ten years. Traditions of the Snohomish Indians, of the Pacific Northwest, recount that long-ago era in the misty haze of antiquity, when the sky hung low and there was no thunder or lightning. Why did the "sky hang low"? Does this suggest that at one time a different atmospheric organization, a different climatological regime existed, providing a more favorable environment for life?

Before examining details further, definitions of two terms are necessary. The term GREENHOUSE EFFECT is used to describe the totality of the earth's atmospheric envelope which apparently prevailed in the pre-flood era. This includes the lower atmosphere (the troposphere) as well as the middle and high atmospheres, the stratosphere, and the ionosphere. This, THE GREENHOUSE EFFECT, included all the mixes of gases throughout the earth's three-tiered atmosphere.

The term ANTEDILUVIAN CANOPY is used to describe only the permanent cloud cover in the lower atmosphere (the troposphere), a cloud cover which may either be described or alluded to in the following Scriptures:

> And God said, Let there be a firmament [atmosphere] in the midst of the waters, and let it divide the waters from the waters. And God made the firmament, and divided the waters which were under the firmament [the oceans] *from the waters which were above the firmament* [the canopy] and it was so (Genesis 1:6-7). When I made the cloud [the canopy] the garment thereof [for the earth], and thick darkness a swaddlingband for it (Job 38:9). "Thou coveredst it with the deep as with a garment: the waters [the canopy] stood above the mountains" (Psalm 104:6).

The permanent cloud cover of the earth, in the model which follows (to the best of our judgment and understanding), may have been 3,000 to 5,000 feet thick, and ranged between 5,000 and 10,000 feet above the earth's sea level.

---

footprint impressions. Man appeared on the scene a mere 1,000,000 evolutionary years ago, whereas, dinosaurs presumably disappeared from the scene about 60,000,000 evolutionary orbits ago. Evolutionary mythology doesn't regard the two as being within 59,000,000 years of each other, much less simultaneous.

Part I

A Model of the Earth's Pre-flood Atmosphere

A study of the earth's atmosphere and its likely ancient Greenhouse Effect can be better understood by looking briefly at the atmospheres of some of the other nearer plants. Two of the planets have no canopies. They are Mercury and Mars. Mercury has no atmosphere because of its small size and mass. Its gravity cannot overcome the kinetic energy of gaseous molecules, and they escape.

In the case of Mars, it does have a rather thin atmosphere, composed primarily of nitrogen and oxygen. There seem to be cloud formations in the atmosphere of this cold planet, particularly (a) in the polar areas in the summer, and (b) in the sunset regions of the lower latitudes. There also seem to be dust storms of high velocity. Since extreme temperature inequities create rapid wind systems, these Martian winds are not surprising. But there is no general cloud cover, and relatively little free water vapor on this barren, frozen planet.

Jupiter and Saturn do not have genuine examples of canopies because a canopy implies that sunlight can penetrate *through* the layer of gas. Upper atmospheric temperatures of Jupiter are around -200° F., which is much too cold for water vapor to be present. It is not to cold for ammonia and methane gases, however. These two gases are abundant in the spectra of both Jupiter and Saturn. There is also good reason to suspect, based on density ratios, that each of these planets has a deep layer of atmosphere, primarily hydrogen, over 10,000 miles thick. Neither the weak sunlight of the distant sun, 500,000,000 miles from Jupiter's orbit, nor even the intense sunlight in Mercury's region, just 28,000,000 miles from the sun, could penetrate such a thick blanket. With atmospheric pressures over 10,000 miles deep, where these Jovian planets do finally have something approaching a core, temperatures are very hot indeed.

One of Saturn's satellites is interesting. It is Titan, a satellite that is larger than either Pluto or Mercury. Titan is massive enough to retain an atmosphere, and methane bands have been recognized in its spectrum.

Venus, of course, is the most interesting planet, for it is our closest neighbor, and it possesses a very brilliant, reflective surface (called an albedo), with a reflecting power of 76 per cent. This may be compared to our earth's albedo of 39 per cent, with its partial cloud cover and its reflective oceans, or it may be compared to our barren non-atmospheric moon with an albedo of 7 per cent. Venus has a rather dense atmosphere, comprised primarily of carbon dioxide. There is also evidence of some water vapor in its lower atmosphere. In the upper, or outer, atmosphere of Venus the intense action of solar ultra-violet radiation upon the abundant carbon dioxide has produced a high level zone, or *canopy*, of carbon suboxide, C_3O_2.

Figures 1, 2, 3, and 4 illustrate our model of the earth's pre-flood Greenhouse Effect. Figure 1 gives prime attention to temperature gradients. The pre-flood atmosphere was comprised, we suspect, of 3 to 5 times as much water vapor as is today's atmosphere. And, like today, this was concentrated in the lower troposphere.

The pre-flood atmosphere is also suspected to have contained

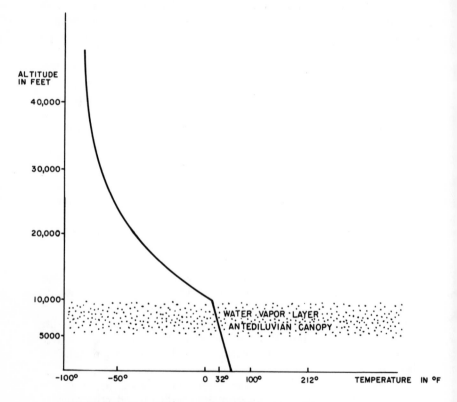

GREENHOUSE MODEL OF PREFLOOD EARTH
TEMPERATURE AND ALTITUDE

FIGURE 1

from 6 to 8 times as much carbon dioxide as the present atmosphere, which is .03 per cent CO_2, diffused in equal proportions throughout the atmosphere. The pre-flood atmosphere is suspected to have contained from .20 to .25 per cent CO_2, and very possibly more. Both carbon dioxide and water vapor are efficient at capturing long wave radiation, which happens to be the kind our planet's crust gives off. Hence, in the lower atmosphere, pre-flood conditions existed in which the earth lost very little of its long wave radiation, its heat. Indeed, it retained almost all. The temperatures of the

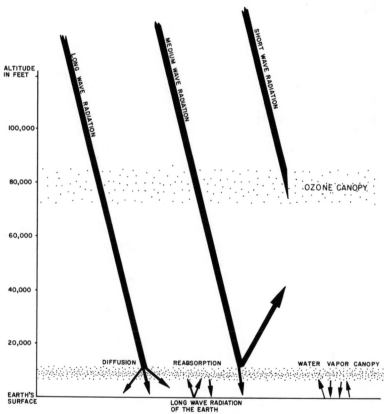

GREENHOUSE MODEL OF PREFLOOD EARTH
LIGHT ABSORPTION, DIFFUSION AND REFLECTION

FIGURE 2

earth's surface, it is suspected, were warm on a pole-to-pole basis, and the oceans were similarly warm in high latitudes as well as in low latitudes. The daily temperature range (the diurnal range) may have been only 2° to 4° F. It was a well-insulated earth in those days, and a well-shielded earth.

Figure 2 is an illustration to show how the earth was lighted by diffused rather than direct light. The earth's reflectivity or albedo at that time may have rivalled that of Venus (76%). Short wave radiation was filtered out through the upper level ozone layer, or ozone canopy, in the ionosphere. (Ozone concentrated in a few parts per million in the upper atmosphere becomes an effective filter for ultraviolet radiation.) Long wave radiation penetrated through the outer ozone canopy and through the intermediary stratosphere. It was partly reflected off, but primarily entered and was diffused through the water vapor canopy in the lower troposphere. The sun's long wave radiation was absorbed; and the earth's long wave radiation was captured, and its heat retained by (and within) the lower canopy.

Figure 3 illustrates Venus, the present Earth, and the pre-flood Earth in terms of the *outer canopy* and the *inner canopy*. The outer canopy is ozone for the Earth, carbon suboxide for Venus. Today the earth has a dilute, or thin but most significant, outer canopy of ozone. Before the flood the ozone canopy was thicker, since ozone is (a) created by short wave solar radiation, and is (b) decomposed by long wave earth or solar radiation. The long wave earth radiation which today plays an important part in reducing the ozone canopy played no such part in the pre-flood era, since the long wave radiation was trapped in the lower atmosphere by the water vapor canopy and the stronger carbon dioxide mix.

Hence, in the pre-flood era the earth had a double canopy, whereas today it has only a dilute, high level single canopy. In the pre-flood era the earth had (a) a thicker and more efficient high level ozone canopy, (b) a thick and efficient low level water vapor canopy, and (c) a more concentrated general mix of carbon dioxide. The inner canopy was a low, unbroken water vapor condition.

Evidence will be presented as to why the pre-flood atmosphere contained *more carbon dioxide* and *more water vapor* than does the present atmosphere. This would logically suggest that the earth's barometric pressure at sea level in the pre-flood era was higher — slightly higher than in the present era.

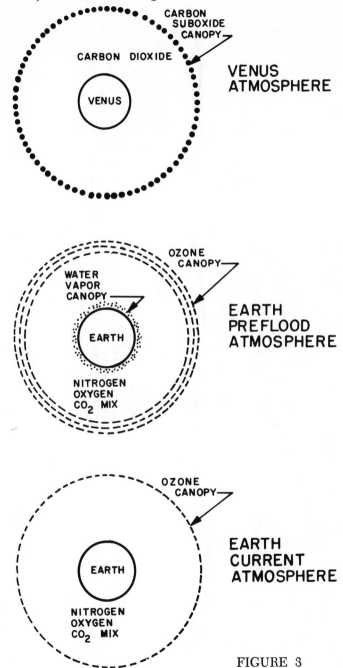

FIGURE 3

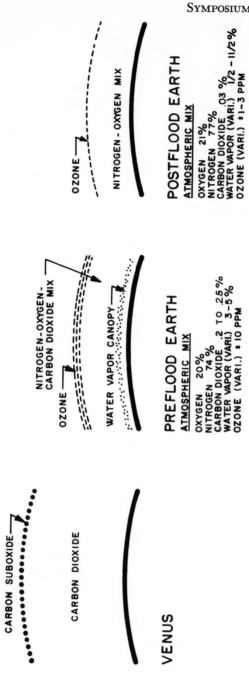

FIGURE 4

POSTFLOOD EARTH

ATMOSPHERIC MIX

OZONE

NITROGEN - OXYGEN MIX

OXYGEN 21%
NITROGEN 77%
CARBON DIOXIDE .03 %
WATER VAPOR (VARI.) 1/2 – 11/2%
OZONE (VARI.) ±1–3 PPM

PREFLOOD EARTH

ATMOSPHERIC MIX

NITROGEN-OXYGEN-
CARBON DIOXIDE MIX

OZONE

WATER VAPOR CANOPY

OXYGEN 20%
NITROGEN 74%
CARBON DIOXIDE .2 TO .25%
WATER VAPOR (VARI.) 3–5%
OZONE (VARI.) ± 10 PPM

CARBON SUBOXIDE

CARBON DIOXIDE

VENUS

TABLE 1

COMPOSITION OF GASES

Gas	Pre-flood Era	Post-flood Era
Nitrogen	74-75%	77%
Oxygen	19-20%	21%
Water Vapor	4-6% (non-variable)	½-1-½% (variable)
Carbon Dioxide	.2 to .25%	.03%
Ozone –		
Lower atmos.	0% (0 ppm.)	.001-.01 parts per million
Upper atmos.	10 ppm.	1-3 ppm.

Changes in mixes of gases in the atmosphere may seem subtle, and possibly irrelevant. The atmosphere only weighs less than one-millionth of the earth's mass, but relatively light or not, here is the life zone, and here is the earth's most exposed and unstable fluid. Relatively small changes in the fluid atmosphere, upon further research, may yield an understanding as to why tropical climates prevailed in now polar regions, or why animals generally grew larger, or why men reportedly lived so long.

Part II

The Existence of the Canopy

Geological Evidence

The existence of both a canopy, and a general greenhouse effect is suggested in the Scriptures, and is deduced from the record in the rocks. There is ample evidence that such parched regions as the Sahara Desert, the Great Australian (Sandy) Desert, the Chilean Atacama Desert, and the deserts of the American West were formerly well-watered, humid, and even swampy regions.

For instance, near Cairo one may find evidence of broad leaf forests which were suddenly entombed and petrified; Cairo today has 3 or 4 inches of rain in one of its wetter years. Again, throughout the dry, arid or semi-arid American West, in such states as Washington, Oregon, Idaho, Utah, Colorado, Arizona, Nevada, and California, as well as Mexican Sonora, we find petrified forests containing broad leaf deciduous trees, coniferous trees, and even palm trees. And the rings in the trees do not suggest slow growth patterns, which dry climates would induce. Rather, the trees were large and fast growing, as was the other associated vegetation.

This suggests that there has been a profound, and perhaps also a
sudden change in *humidity* in these formerly well-watered regions.
A climate may be measured in terms of humidity. For instance,
the interior of Antarctica may qualify as a desert, even though
frozen water abounds. It receives about as much annual precipitation as does the Sahara Desert, but in a much different temperature range, and hence evaporation ratio. *Humidity changes*
are one thing, and *temperature changes* are another. Have there
also been dramatic, profound and sudden climatic changes in
terms of temperature? Concerning Arctic conditions, observe:

> The luxuriant growth of broad leaf hardwood forests in high
> Arctic latitudes persisted . . . indicating a prolonged continuation
> of humid, warm temperature, or at least temperate forest climates
> in polar regions. Evidence for this may be found in both Artic
> and Antarctic regions.[3]

> The rock fragments from this mountainside invariably included
> plant fossils, leaf and stem impressions, coal and fossilized wood.
> Here at the southernmost known mountain in the world, scarcely
> two hundred miles from the South Pole, was found conclusive
> evidence that the climate of Antarctica was once temperate or even
> sub-tropical.[4]

In the Yukon Territory of Canada, so celebrated in the works
of Robert Service for its harsh, long and dark winters, its icy
blasts and hardy miners, sub-tropical lotus seeds have been found
imbedded in frozen ground. This illustrates that the frozen
Yukon once had a climate similar to Formosa, Okinawa, Kyushu or
Shikoku, and possibly as tropical as the Philippine Islands.

Equally conclusive, and perhaps more dramatic is the evidence
which suggests that serene, Siberian mammoths and rhinos, grazing
on sub-tropical or temperate vegetation, marbled in fat, surrounded
by sedges, berry bushes, and fruit trees, were suddenly plunged not
merely into freezing conditions, but into conditions so cold that they
were lethal to animals, clad in fur, weighing many tons. Baron Toll
was credited with the discovery of at least two mammoths, in
1885 and 1886, among the now frigid islands north of Siberia.

> Baron Edward Toll, the explorer, reported finding a fallen 90-foot
> fruit tree with ripe fruit and green leaves still on its branches, in

[3]Hooker, Dolph E., *Those Astounding Ice Ages*, New York; Exposition
    Press, 1948, p. 44.
[4]*Loc. cit.*

the frozen ground of the New Siberian Islands. The only tree vegetation that grows there now is the one-inch high willow.[5]

Evolutionary-uniformitarian theorists have supposed that no global catastrophes have occurred; their framework does not allow for such — all changes were gradual. (The present is the key to the past, they presume.) Consider the problems that the uniformitarians and evolutionists have with the Beresovka mammoth, whose carcass now resides in a St. Petersburg museum. It contains the following features:

1. The tusks. Colagen, a gelatin compound found in the tusks and lips, decomposes at temperatures at or above freezing. Little of the gelatin in these tusks has decomposed or dissolved since burial, illustrating both perfect preservation and *permanent* frozen conditions since the time of sudden, freezing death.

2. The digestive tract. Within the digestive tract were found tender sedges, partly undigested, and partly still green. Twenty-seven pounds of vegetation, all of sub-tropical or mild temperate types (according to the best translations from the Russian) were found in one portion of the intestinal region. Grasses with seeds were also found, suggesting death came with suddenness (green grass, and sedges, not dried and/or withered vegetation).

3. The mouth. This also contained unswallowed and partly masticated grass, indicating that death came with instant suddenness.

4. The muscular tissue. The mammoths were not scrawny individuals; they were larger than any current pachyderms. They were marbled in fat and weighed many tons. Birds-eye frozen food experts, in examining the mammoth tissue, have deduced that they were "thrown in the cooler" suddenly, into temperatures below -150°F. The water separation within the cell proceeds at death, and ceases at freezing. The time differential between death and freezing allowed for little separation even in the interior portions of these beasts, and this condition is the basis for temperature estimates at and after death.

5. The reproductive system. The Beresovka mammoth was a male, and this male was quick-frozen with an erection. (Incidentally, this occurs to men immediately after electrocution, and may possibly be a clue as to the nature of the sudden demise and permafrost entombment of the mammoths.) This is another difficult problem for the slow-freeze, slow-snow evolutionary uniformitarians.

---

[5]Charles Hapgood, "The Mystery of the Frozen Mammoths," *Coronet*, Sept. 1960, p. 74.

There are other problems, such as associated fruit trees with green leaves, and even ripe fruit in these regions in the permafrost. There are quick-frozen pachyderms in some regions, and apparently almost simultaneous quick-drowned pachyderms in other regions, requiring some kind of catastrophic synchronization.

Herein are presented just some bits of geological evidence that climates have changed both suddenly and dramatically, and in varying degrees of permanence, and such changes are in terms of both (a) *temperature*, and (b) *humidity*. The whole problem, of course, is more complex than merely a concern with atmospheric temperatures. As was previously noted, tropical marine crustaceans are found in high Arctic latitudes suggesting there has also been a profound drop in oceanic temperatures. A former luxuriant, moderate climate has been turned, in some areas, into parched deserts, and in other areas into conditions of permanent ice and snow. These climatic changes are best understood if we conceive that the earth once had a temperate to sub-tropical climate from pole to pole, a planetary temperature equilibrium, in short, a Greenhouse Effect.

Evolutionary-uniformitarians, geocentric rather than celestial in their views, tend to look downward for all changes, supposed to be gradual and slow. They fail to look upward for catastrophes, into the planetary realms, where evidence of past catastrophes sweep across the celestial scene. They exist literally from Mercury to Pluto, and do not exclude the asteroids, battered fragments of a former planet, or the Rings of Saturn, evidence of a second icy cataclysm in our solar system.[6] Evolutionary-uniformitarians assume that the earth's North Pole could hardly have changed location within the last 5,000 to 7,000 years, merely because their framework of geocentric thought allows no room for such possibilities.

This article does not yield to such a non-catastrophic presumption. Indeed, if the flood was by nature tidal, it was indeed an astronomical catastrophe, likely of some five months duration. Such a celestial disaster necessarily would have wrought many effects on the earth system, including: (1) a change in the location of the earth's geographical poles; (2) a change in the tilt of the earth's axis; (3) a change in the eccentricity of the earth's orbit; (4) a change in the distance of the earth's orbit from the sun.

One may expand his mental horizon by considering celestial

[6]Patten, Donald W., *The Biblical Flood and the Ice Epoch*, Seattle, Washington, Pacific Meridian Publishing Co., 1966, pp. 27-50, 137-193, 277-308.

catastrophism side by side with a little catastrophic cosmology such as occurs in Job 9:

> God, Which removeth the mountains, and they know not,
> Which overtaketh them in his anger,
> Which shaketh the earth out of her place, and the pillars thereof tremble,
> Which commandeth the sun, and it riseth not . . .
> Which doeth great things past finding out,
> yea, wonders without number.

Job 38:37b:
> Who can stay the bottles [planets] of heaven.

The vast subject of the past catastrophic interaction or engagement and disengagement of the earth with forces of astronomical dimension is further suggested in Job 38:32, 33:

> Canst thou bring forth Mazzaroth [a sort of wild card planet in the solar system] in his season? or canst thou guide Arcturus with his sons? Knowest thou the ordinances of heaven? canst thou set the dominion thereof in the earth?

Hence, while evolutionary-uniformitarians may make assumptions and suppositions of a serene astronomical past for the earth for any number of hypothetical millions of years, and while they may view the earth in isolation to its primary celestial environment, such assumptions must no longer be allowed to pass. The solar system, as a major environment, with a historic catastrophic potential from Mercury to Pluto and beyond, must be conceived within the catastrophic framework of thought.

Back to our planet, changes in *weather* are one matter, and sudden and permanent changes in *climate* are another. Humidity differentials are one factor within a climate. They are to be considered apart from (but concomitant with) temperature changes among other climatological factors. If there was a Greenhouse Effect embracing the planet Earth, then moderate, warm, subtropical temperatures and a constantly high relative humidity would have been a global phenomenon, of which more shall be considered later.

Part III

Scriptural Indications of the Pre-flood Canopy

1. The Visible Water Vapor Canopy, or Water Vapor Gauze in the Atmosphere:

> And God said, Let there be a firmament [atmosphere] in the midst of the waters, and let it divide the waters from the waters.

And God made the firmament [the atmosphere], and divided the
waters which were under the firmament [lakes, seas, swamps,
oceans] *from the waters which were above the firmament* [the
water vapor canopy], and it was so (Genesis 1:6-7).

Where wast thou when I laid the foundations of the earth? de-
clare if thou hast understanding. Who hath laid the measures
thereof, if thou knowest? or who hath stretched a line upon it?
*When I made the cloud the garment thereof, and thick darkness
a swaddlingband for it* (Job 38:4, 5, 9).

Comment: The "swaddlingband of the earth" is a term of translation describing this ancient condition, even as the Snohomish
Indians called it a time when "the sky hung low." In the Genesis
account the "firmament" suggests in English terra firma, but its
meaning is quite different. It means "atmosphere." The waters below the firmament were the hydrography, the lakes, oceans, seas
and swamps. The waters above the firmament comprised the canopy.

2. The Altitude of the Canopy and the Thickness of the Canopy:

When he prepared the heavens, I was there: when he set a compass upon the face of the depth.
When he established the clouds above: when he strengthened the
fountains of the deep (Proverbs 8:27-28).

Comment: In our current atmospheric arrangement, temperature
declines as one ascends into the atmosphere, since pressure dimin-
ishes. The decline in temperature is termed the "adiabatic rate,"
and is between 3° and 3.5° per 1,000 feet. We suspect that the
sea level surface temperature of much of the earth before the
flood was between 60° and 70° F. At 10,000 feet in altitude, it was
between 25° and 35° F. In 5,000 feet temperatures will drop about
15° to 18° F. It is proposed that the water vapor canopy was
3,000 to 5,000 feet thick, and ranged between 5,000 and 10,000 feet
above sea level.

Some have proposed that the canopy must have been many
miles thick, since there were forty days and nights of rain to condense out at the onset of the flood. This is a misunderstanding
for several reasons. First, sunlight could not penetrate such a
thick canopy. Secondly, if all of the current atmosphere were
saturated at 1-½ per cent to 3 per cent concentration (with
15 pounds of pressure per square inch) this would comprise, or
condense out, between 10 and 18 inches of rain per square inch of
earth surface. This is not much of a flood. Thirdly, it has been

suggested that an ice epoch dump, a catastrophic dump, occurred (a) simultaneously with the onset of the flood, and (b) over the magnetic, or auroral regions. The source of the rain was not atmospheric condensation primarily, but rather was low latitude slop-over of the ice dump. Ice particles provided the nuclei of condensation to sweep out the pre-flood· canopy. Fourth, the source of water for the flood has also been demonstrated to be the oceans, surging in tidal formations, under conditions of earth deformation, the suggested "fountains of the deep" which surged for 150 days in the Genesis account. Hence, the proposal for a thick canopy is neither logical nor necessary.

3. The Pre-flood Temperature Equilibrium (which caused a lack of planetary wind systems, in turn causing a lack of rain, but in its stead, *a planetary dew regime*).

> And every plant of the field before it was in the earth, and every herb of the field before it grew, for the Lord God had not caused it to rain upon the earth, and there was not a man to till the ground. But there went up a mist from the earth, and watered the whole face of the ground (Genesis 2:5, 6).

Comment: This observation states that there was (1) a total and universal absence of rain in the pre-flood world. It also directly suggests that there was (2) a daily or diurnal dew regime, based on humidity, saturation, temperature, dewpoint, and condensation.

Both of these suggest a lack of planetary wind systems. For instance, dew will form only in the absence of wind. But more important, in today's climatic regime, whichever type of rain may fall, be it orographic, cyclonic, or convective, it is caused by one or more types of winds. *Winds cause rain.* But what causes winds? Temperature differentials across the earth's surface cause wind systems both on a local scale and on a global scale. Today the earth's atmosphere may be described as one vast wind machine, endeavoring to moderate the recurring temperture differentials across the latitudes and landforms.

For instance, today over the great continent Eurasia monsoons occur seasonally. This great continent heats up more rapidly than the surrounding oceans in the summer. Hot air rises and draws in cooler maritime air across the continental peripheries (edges). This cooler, maritime air happens to be humid, and it is termed the summer monsoon, with its warm, rain-bearing winds.

In the winter the reverse occurs. Cold, dead, heavy, polar air builds up over the frozen continent because the planet's crust gives off much heat, while receiving but little from the sun. These cold polar air masses become very heavy, build up and burst out of the center of Siberia. It is extremely cold and dry air. Thus, with a change in seasons and a change in the relative temperatures of land masses, the direction of the winds reverse. The quality of the winds sharply changes both in humidity and in temperature. This is a seasonal wind system.

However, let us discuss further the pre-flood Greenhouse Effect. The long wave radiation of the earth was captured and retained by (1) the low level water vapor canopy and by (2) a higher carbon dioxide mix throughout the atmosphere. With a Greenhouse Effect the low level canopy reflected much light and diffused the balance. The earth did not gain a great deal of heat during the daytime, nor did it lose much at night. A temperature equilibrium or near equilibrium was established.

Humidity naturally rose to near saturation or the saturation level. When night came, temperatures dropped 2 or 3 degrees. Dewpoint was reached, and a thick layer of nocturnal dew was formed. During the day with an absence of dry, desiccating winds, evaporation was slow. The earth was well watered, both from the perspective of an abundance of condensation and a lethargy in evaporation. Swamps were abundant, but parched deserts of frigid tundras were not to be found in such a dew regime.[7]

Along with temperature, *evaporation* as well as *precipitation* is an essential to measure post-flood climates. For instance, today 10 inches of rainfall and/or snow is sufficient to grow a crop of wheat in a cool, brief summer of Saskatchewan, whereas 25 inches of rain may be quite insufficient in the hot, arid, parched climate of West Texas. The reason for the greater efficiency of the precipitation in Saskatchewan is the lower evaporation ratio. Before the flood, with (1) the canopy, (2) a nearly saturated atmosphere and (3) a temperature equilibrium, the evaporation rate was similarly

---

[7] It may be of interest to the reader to note another type of artificial Greenhouse Effect, under experimental research by the Kwick-Lok Industries, Inc., of Yakima, Washington. Here barley seeds are experimentally laid out in pans in a type of large enclosed walk-in freezer type container. There are four small flourescent tubes, one in each corner. The trays of barley seed are kept under conditions of saturation and warm constant temperature. They are sprayed with water and nutrients six times daily. Under these conditions barley is seen to grow *9 to 11 inches high in 7 days, without sunlight and without soil.* This can theoretically be done in Alaska as easily as in California. This is an artificial Greenhouse Effect, bearing a few resemblances to the pre-flood world, where diurnal condensation and a permanent cloud cover pervaded.

very subdued. Hence, a rainless earth would be, and was, a well-watered environment (habitat).[8]

> And they heard the voice of the Lord God walking in the garden in the *cool of the day*; and Adam and his wife hid themselves from the presence of the Lord God amongst the trees of the garden (Genesis 3:8).

Superficially, the "cool of the day" is a strange phrase in the pre-flood era of the Greenhouse Effect, with its reduced diurnal (daily) temperature range. With the coming of dusk and the dropping of temperature 2 to 3 degrees, the nearly saturated atmosphere again became saturated, as dewpoint was reached. Condensation formed. A chilling layer of dew occurred. This, we suspect, was the "chill of the day" or the "cool of the day." This phrase does not refer to gross temperature decline, but, rather to dewpoint and condensation.

4. The Visibility of the Canopy and Its Sudden Collapse:

> In the six hundredth year of Noah's life, in the second month, the seventeenth day of the month, the same day were all the fountains of the great deep broken up, *and the windows of heaven were opened* (Genesis 7:11).

Comment: It has previously been noted how essential it is to understand the relationship between the flood, or tidal or gravitational phenomenon, and the ice dump, an electro-magnetic phenomenon. Both were simultaneous. With the intrusion of ice particles through the magnetosphere and ionosphere into the lower troposphere, the ideal nuclei of condensation were suddenly provided. The canopy was cleaned out, and in a matter of hours. With its sudden departure came the sudden presentation of blue, blue sky. The windows of the atmospheric heavens appeared. The canopy was dissolved, or collapsed, the same day as the onset of the flood. The (blue) windows of heaven were opened.

The Scriptures suggest that the ark was already loaded with its human and animal cargo. Undoubtedly, the earth's crust was already shuddering and quaking from preliminary deformation.[8] The same day of the flotation of the ark was the dissolution of the canopy, the seventh day of that chaotic period.

> And the windows of heaven were opened. And the rain was upon the earth 40 days and 40 nights (Genesis 7:11b-12). . . . 150 days later . . .

---

[8]Patten, Donald W., *op. cit.*, pp. 63-64.

And God remembered Noah and every living thing, and all the cattle that were with him in the ark, *and God made a wind to pass over the earth,* and the waters assuaged (Genesis 8:1).

Comment: The establishment of the new, post-flood climate was based on a *new atmospheric organization.* The former low level water vapor in the troposphere had condensed out and vanished. In its stead were irregular, swirling cyclonic fronts of cloud systems frequenting certain latitudes and not frequenting other latitudes. A permanent heat disequilibrium of the planet's surface became the new norm. Direct sunlight shone across the latitudes and onto the crust at varying angles, heating the surface quite unequally.

(In addition, we deduce, a vast dump of ice on the two magnetic polar regions had been accomplished with 40 days of suddenness, and comprising ice well under -150° F., possibly under -200° F. This sudden ice dump covered some 20,000,000 square miles of area in each hemisphere. Massive ice flow and scouring commenced, surrounding and engulfing such mountains as the 5,000-foot Adirondacks. Mammoths became drowned and buried suddenly in sediments in some regions, and suddenly mummified in ice in the Siberian region. All of this ice and its subsequent melt added to the temperature disequilibriums both in the atmosphere and in the hydrosphere. Tropical marine crustaceans may continue to thrive in some places, but not in the Arctic Ocean.)[9, 10]

It may be of more than passing interest to note something in the brief account in Genesis at the end of the flood, 8:1b, "And God made a wind to pass over the earth." A temperature disequilibrium, so absent from the pre-flood scene, is now so prominent, as are its resultant wind systems (cf. Job 38:29-30).

Temperature differentials, wind systems with the rain-bearing moistures, and/or their drying, desiccating effects were a part of the aftermath of the flood, as were outflowing ice masses. The fountains of the deep, the oceans, had ceased their surging. The 150 tragic, chaotic days of tides, rapid sedimentation, crustal deformation, massive ice dumps, and atmospheric reorganization were over — to say nothing of a probable polar relocation, a likely shift in axial tilt, and a likely orbital perturbation, with a new 91.5 and 94.5 million mile perihelion and aphelion orbit.[11]

[9]Morris, Henry M., *et al*, *A Symposium on Creation* (I), Grand Rapids, Michigan, Baker Book House, 1968, p. 119-135.

[10]Patten, Donald W., *op. cit.*, pp. 101-136.

[11]Patten, Donald W., *Evangelical Flood Cosmologies*, Seattle, Washington, Pacific Meridian Publishing Co., 1968, pp. 27-31.

Through all of this Noah remained something of a thirtieth century non-conformist — also something of a thirtieth century B.C. conservative. Two great tidal crescendoes had nearly destroyed the planet. He was not positive that everything was over. He remained in the ark another 210 days, just to be safe, and sent out some winged observers from time to time. Then he, his wife, his sons, and his daughters-in-law disembarked into the new era, a new and lonely, and, we are confident, a relatively windy world.

5. Increase in the Level of Actinic (Short Wave) Radiation:

With the water vapor canopy gone, more short wave radiation, such as is in the ultra-violet range, bathed the earth's surface. Did this tend, or was it something else that tended to affect life in some mysterious way to shorten growth periods, and to shorten life spans? If so, how?

The Book of Genesis presents some rather astounding, extensive, and significant analysis on the ages of the patriarchs, both before and after the flood. This includes the "beget" and "begot" chapters of Genesis which may possibly bore a beginning reader. This theme will be discussed in greater detail later in this chapter and by Dr. McCone, in a later chapter. For the moment only the possibility of a change in atmosphere and a shortened life span for man is observed. Subtle or not in terms of atmospheric physics this is perhaps the most important — certainly one of the more important of all — of the changes between the pre-flood and the post-flood era, at least for man.

If the earth during the Greenhouse Effect era was so luxuriant and life-filled and bountiful, why? What was the pre-flood atmosphere like? How did the climatology work to effect gigantism in animals? How did the climatology work to effect a longevity for the human race? Why did men live for nine centuries before the flood? Partial answers may come from a more detailed analysis of the Greenhouse Effect.

Part IV

The Composition of the Pre-flood "Greenhouse Effect" Atmosphere

Previously it was suggested that there was more water vapor and more carbon dioxide in the pre-flood atmosphere.

Water Vapor

With a temperature equilibrium and a greenhouse effect, the normal tendency toward saturation by water vapor of the lower atmosphere proceeded unhindered by wind systems or rain. The troposphere of the earth contained perhaps three to five times as much total water vapor as does the current atmospheric envelope. Today barometric pressure at sea level is about 15 pounds per square inch. Before the flood it may have been within the range of 16 to 18 pounds, also producing a slight warming effect.

Carbon Dioxide

One may deduce there was more carbon dioxide in the pre-flood atmosphere for several reasons:

(1) The greater richness of plant life, even in such locations as Alaska, Antarctica, Siberia, and the Yukon indicate a greater availability and presence of pre-flood carbon. Much of the pre-flood carbon in flora and fauna became buried by flood waters and alluvium, and it became locked into sedimentary carbonates, no longer available to the biosphere.

(2) Limestone ($CaCO_3$) and dolomite ($CaMg (CO_3)_2$ form a large portion of the stratigraphic record. Much of this may be due to primordial catastrophe or catastrophes. Yet some more may have precipitated during the flood catastrophe. Vast amounts of carbon have been withdrawn via solution and precipitation during these past earth events.

(3) A reservoir of carbon in petroleum pools and natural gas collections were generally closer to the surface in the pre-flood era. It may be of interest to note that some geologists are beginning to suspect that some hydrocarbons may have an extra-terrestrial source, and a catastrophic arrival to our planet in a primordial catastrophic era.

(4) Temperatures of the pre-flood oceans were warmer, as is illustrated by tropical crustaceans fossilized in Arctic regions. Antarctic fossils show similar temperature ranges. Today's oceans contain about 90 per cent of the carbon dioxide which circulates between the atmosphere, fauna, flora, and oceans. Atmosphere, fauna and flora contain a collective 10 per cent. Warmer oceans cannot dissolve as much carbon dioxide as cold oceans. It is something like the temperature of soda water. At cool temperatures soda water can retain much more dissolved CO_2 than when warm. The same is true with the oceans. In the pre-flood era the volume of carbon dioxide dissolved in the warmer oceans was lower, and hence the volume of carbon dioxide in the atmosphere was greater.

Thus, by three mechanisms, namely, by burial, by precipitation, and by dissolving in colder oceans, pre-flood carbon became locked out of the post-flood biosphere. The pre-flood atmosphere may have contained .2 to .1 per cent carbon dioxide. Conservatively, we suggest it was at least over .1 per cent. Table 1, page 19, recounts this estimate.

Concerning water vapor, it does not mix equally throughout the atmosphere due to lower temperatures in the stratosphere, where water vapor cannot be retained. Concerning carbon dioxide, however, it diffuses equally throughout the atmosphere and it is also particularly efficient at capturing long wave radiation. Whether the increase in carbon dioxide in the pre-flood atmosphere was more significant in the Greenhouse Effect than was the low level water vapor canopy is a moot point. The high carbon dioxide mix in the pre-flood atmosphere may well be the basic reason why the water vapor canopy did not burn off or dissipate.

Part V

Carbin-14 Dating

Today in our upper atmosphere, the ionosphere, the intense cosmic rays from outer space enter into the earth's atmosphere and occasionally a particle will strike a nitrogen nucleus, causing a loss of an electron, which converts the nitrogen into heavy carbon, or carbon-14. This promptly reacts with oxygen to become carbon dioxide, but not of the regular C-12 variety.

When Libby presented the C-14 dating scheme, many of his assumptions and analyses were correct. For instance, he assumed that the half life of C-14 was 5600 years, which was close enough. Its presence in a non-renewable state in dead organic material did provide a clear potential and a new horizon for dating schemes.

Libby made nine assumptions in his dating scheme — five of which seem to us to be correct. But, unfortunately, Libby subconsciously made some uniformitarian assumptions which merit scrutiny and rejection. Libby assumed a constancy in the earth system during the last 100,000 years, a subconscious uniformitarianism, for the following:

(1) The Circulation of the Atmosphere: He failed to consider the pre-flood Greenhouse Effect in which a temperature equilibrium prevailed, and in which there were very little in the way of winds, both horizontal and vertical wind systems. We suggest there were no convection currents. C-14, manufactured in the upper atmosphere, largely remained there and accumulated. This accumulation began to mix into lower atmosphere, the troposphere, only after the flood, with newly developed wind systems.

(2)   The Mix of Carbon Dioxide in the Atmosphere: For reasons
      already presented we estimate the mix of carbon dioxide
      in the pre-flood atmosphere at between .2 and .25 per cent,
      and there is a possibility of a mix as high as .3 to .4 per cent.
      Libby assumed the mix was .03 per cent for the pre-flood
      era, because he recognized nothing in terms of a global,
      planetary flood cataclysm.

(3)   Constancy of Oceanic Temperatures: Libby assumed oceanic
      temperatures, in which today the great reservoir of available
      carbon dioxide is dissolved, to be like they were today some
      100,000 years ago. Today it is recognized that this can
      hardly be the case due to the ice epoch (ice age). Nobody
      seriously endeavors to C-14 date beyond the ice epoch, al-
      though no evolutionary uniformitarian understands either the
      dating or the mechanism of the ice dump.[12] It must be
      added that since the preliminary scheme was proposed,
      Libby has developed serious reservations himself about the
      aforementioned three assumptions.

(4)   The C-14 Disequilibrium: It is estimated that it takes 30,000
      years for the accumulation of C-14 to produce a decay rate
      which will equal the manufacture rate.[13] Originally Libby
      assumed that there was such an equilibrium between decay
      and manufacture. (Why not?) However, *the equilibrium
      has not yet been achieved.* In fact, the present decay rate
      approximates only 70 per cent of the manufacture rate.
      There is one seemingly direct answer to this circumstance,
      namely, that the current nitrogen mix has not been in our
      earth's atmosphere for 30,000 years. Ten thousand or 15,000
      years of atmospheric nitrogen mix would more nearly fit the
      circumstance. A catastrophe in the primeval period such
      as is suggested in Genesis 1:2, involving capture of am-
      monia, methane and hydrogen, some 8,000 to 20,000 years
      ago, fits in well with the C-14 disequilibrium. How do the
      evolutionary uniformitarians meet this problem? Will their
      framework of thought be pliable enough to adjust for such?
      How then will they answer this problem, if they respond at
      all? This will be very interesting, indeed, to observe.

It must be added that C-14 dating has been tested on artifacts
of known historical dates, and the margin of error climbs to signifi-

---

[12]Patten, Donald W., *op. cit.*, p. 101-136, 277-280.

[13]Cook, Melvin A., "Radiological Dating and Some Pertinent Applications
    of Historical Interest, Do Radiological 'Clocks' Need Repair," *Crea-
    tion Research Society Quarterly*, Vol. 5, No. 2, Sept. 1968, p. 69.

cant proportions for materials older than 2,500 years, or materials older than 500 B.C. Dr. Chittick, author of the next article, holds that when the aforementioned assumptions 1, 2, and 3 of Libby, regarding uniformitarian earth history, are exchanged or substituted out in favor of catastrophic assumptions regarding the flood, the chronicles of Genesis harmonize and merge with a *Revised Catastrophic C-14 Dating Schedule.*

Ice dumps three miles deep over the North Magnetic Pole. . . ice dumps 5,000 feet below sea level in Antarctica . . . quick-frozen mammoths . . . ice and lava formations interleaved or sandwiched together . . . radial ice flow patterns . . . volcanic ash intermixed with ice 5,000 feet below sea level — all of these are facts. Yet, nowhere within popular (uniformitarian) geology has a comprehensible explanation been tendered. But then, popularity does come and go. Perhaps uniformitarianism will, too.

We propose that in the placid, non-circulating pre-flood atmosphere a buildup of C-14 occurred which suddenly mixed with flora and fauna in abnormal proportions. The implication of just this variable in atmospheric mix must be reassessed in order to come up with a realistic dating schedule.

C-14 is a product of the upper atmosphere where the withering, direct, unshielded rays of the sun interact with the outer atmosphere. This is the same region where, on Venus, short wave radiation produces the abnormal high level canopy of carbon suboxide. Are there any other significant developments in the upper atmosphere of the earth which, possibly subtly, possibly profoundly, affect the atmosphere? We think so.

Part VI

Ozone and the Ozone Canopy

Like C-14 and carbon suboxide, ozone is manufactured in upper atmospheres. Where carbon dioxide is abundant, as in Venus's atmosphere, carbon suboxide is the product. Where oxygen is abundant, as in the Earth's atmosphere, ozone in dilute proportions is formed. Ozone is created when an oxygen molecule (O_2) is split by short wave radiation. The individual oxygen atoms recombine into an abnormal form of oxygen, ozone (O_3). Chemically, C-14 reacts just like the normal C-12. Chemically, *ozone does not react just like the normal oxygen molecule.*

In the twentieth century atmospheric environment ozone exists in the upper atmosphere in levels of about one to three parts per million.

Ozone is not distributed uniformly through the atmosphere, but is mostly concentrated between 10 and 40 km above the earth's surface, with a fairly sharp peak in distribution at about 20-30 km.[14]

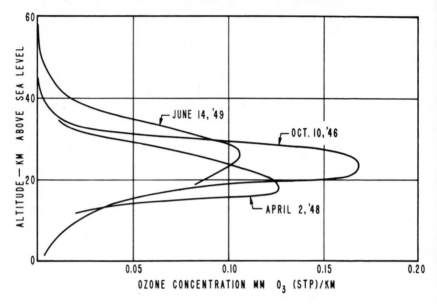

Vertical distribution of O_3 from three NRL rocket flights (Johnson, Purcell, Watanabe, and Tousey, 1952).

From Gerard Kuiper, *The Earth as a Planet,* University of Chicago Press, 1954, p. 439.

FIGURE 5

Ozone in manufactured by short wave radiation in the upper atmosphere. But one might ask, "How does it decay or decrease?" Does it constantly increase or build up? The answer is no. Whereas, it is manufactured by short wave radiation, it is similarly re-converted or catalyzed back into the normal oxygen (O_2) by *long wave radiation,* such as the sun provides, and particularly such as the earth's crust gives off. The re-conversion of ozone back into oxygen is achieved with *increasing efficiency* as ozone circulates, or fluxes, downward toward the crust. At sea level today it will vary from one to three parts per 100,000,000, varying somewhat with prevailing winds, magnetic storms, and closeness to high magnetic

---

[14]Kuiper, Gerard P., *The Earth as a Planet,* Chicago, University of Chicago Press, 1954, p. 439.

latitudes. What effect could such a dilute gas as a few parts per million have upon the earth's outer atmosphere?

> The ozone layer is thus a buffer between the continuance of terrestrial life as we know it at present and sudden extinction by the short wave rays of the Sun, against which we have no physiological protection.[15]

> Sunlight, unfiltered by ozone, is rich in the potent ultraviolet rays which rupture chemical bonds in protoplasm and thereby destroy life. Life exists on earth now only because we are shielded from direct ultraviolet rays by a dilute but extremely essential high level blanket of ozone which our atmosphere provides.[16]

Hence, we may realistically hold that in today's atmosphere the Earth *does possess a canopy*, though unseen by the human eye (which sees only wave lengths between 3,000 and 8,000 Å). Today we have a very thin canopy, a very high one, but a very crucial one.

Now let us consider the low level water vapor canopy of Figures 1, 2, 3, and 4. The low level water vapor canopy efficiently captured long wave radiation, which otherwise would convert ozone back to oxygen. An increased abundance of carbon dioxide would do the same thing. Hence, in a Greenhouse Effect structure of the atmoshere, a considerable amount of long wave radiation was filtered out in the lower atmosphere, allowing for a *lower reconversion rate* of ozone to oxygen. This in turn would result in a thicker high level ozone canopy — one in which no wind systems brought dilute amounts to the surface. We propose that the pre-flood ozone canopy was (a) thicker in the upper atmosphere by a considerable amount, and more concentrated, and was also (b) slightly higher in elevation due to a greater barometric pressure in the pre-flood era.

The Physiological Effects of Ozone

Ozone in our atmosphere, the atmosphere you and I breathe, contains a few parts of ozone per hundred million. This is increased in metropolitan areas. It is increased in strato-cruisers or submarines and in some manufacturing environments. It is increased in or near x-ray laboratories, or arc-welding locations, or

---

[15]Smart, W. N., *The Origin of the Earth*, Baltimore, Penguin Books, 1959, p. 56.
[16]Howe, George F. Unpublished Paper. *Creationistic Botany Today: A Progress Report*, 1969, 24635 Apple St., Newhall, Calif. It is anticipated that this paper will be published in Symposium on Creation III, scheduled for release in early 1971.

cyclotrons. What could a few parts per hundred million of ozone do to the human physiology?

Perhaps this could be better answered by asking what a few parts per million does to human, or animal physiologies. Ozone is an unstable, corrosive, and highly reactive gas, bluish in color in thick layers. Ozone has been measured as high as 11 ppm in the stratosphere, from which there is a steady downward flux due to wind systems into the troposphere, where it is destroyed by catalytic reactions, chemical and photochemical reactions. Its effects on a number of plant species, as an oxidant, is singly harmful. At .05 to .1 ppm its odor becomes pronounced.

A study of 11 subjects exposed to .6 to .8 ppm ozone for one two-hour exposure resulted in a significant reduction in lung diffusing capacity. After-effects involved bronchial irritation and soreness, and a slight dry cough lasting 12 to 24 hours. At a higher concentration of 1.5 to 2.0 ppm, also for a single two-hour exposure, the result was general morbidity lasting two weeks, accompanied by impaired lung function, chest pain, coughing and extreme fatigue.

When humans breathed in 1 ppm ozone for 10 minutes, a decrease in oxygen consumption occurred, plus the sphering of red blood cells. Other findings indicate that ozone may produce secondary effects on body metabolism, damage to myocardial tissue, lung adenomas and general aging effects.

Ozone has been found to be lethal to laboratory animals in concentrations of 3.6 to 20 ppm within several hours. Ozone in lesser concentrations is found to be closely related to increasing mortality rates for laboratory animals.[17]

---

[17]Jaffe, Louis S., "The Biological Effects of Ozone on Man and Animals," *American Industrial Hygiene Association Journal*, May-June, 1967, pp. 267-276.

Prolonged ozone exposures of animals have caused (1) chronic pulmonary injury to lung tissue including bronchiolitis, and emphysematous and fibrotic changes in lung parenchyma, (2) agina, and (3) lung tumor acceleration. Ozone exposures of .1 to .2 ppm, 7 hours per day for 3 weeks caused an increase in mortality of newborn mice.

Significantly increased mortality and severe chronic lung injury including hemorrhage, fibrosis of the lung parenchyma and constriction of the lung airways of guinea pigs and rats occurred after intermittent prolonged exposure of 1.0 ppm ozone, 6 hours per day, 5 days a week for 62 weeks.

Concentrations of 1.5 to 2.0 ppm, beyond the maximum ozone level currently found in community photochemical smog within the range sometimes found in occupational exposures, a single two-hour ozone exposure caused general morbidity in a man lasting for approximately

Increased aging effects of ozone in concentration of parts per ten million are interesting. It is also of interest to note that radiologists, physicians, who often avoid x-ray technician operations,

---

two weeks. His immediate symptoms included impaired lung function, severe chest pains, altered taste sensation, coughing and extreme fatigue.

Ozone is also highly injurious to vegetation.

At .015 ppm it was detectable by most normal people. At .1 ppm, a dryness of the upper respiratory mucosa occurred, irritating to mucous membrances of nose and throat.

At .2 ppm, single 3-hour exposures, considerable decrease of visual acuity in the scotopic and mesoptic ranges occurred. . . .

At .2 ppm, single 6-hour exposure, the sphering of red blood cells was noted in mice, rats, rabbits, and man.

At 1.0 ppm, 4-hour exposure, engorged blood vessels occurred in the lung, with a conspicuous number of leukocytes in the capillaries of mice.

At 1.0 ppm, 6-hour exposure with superimposed cycled exercise patterns for 15 minutes of each hour, 6 of 10 younger rats died of pulmonary edema and hemorrhage, while 5 of 10 older rats died under the same condition.

At 4.0 ppm, single 4-hour exposure, 6 of 8 young mice were killed, while 0 of 8 old mice died.

.2 ppm, 17 weeks of continuous exposure to ozone and tuberculosis, a 60 per cent increase in mortality occurred in ozone-exposed guinea pigs.

.8 to 1.7, chronic occupation exposure by welders resulted in a "disagreeable" odor, dryness of the mouth after a short exposure, with dryness of the mouth and throat, smarting of eyes, tightness of the chest, difficulty in breathing, wheezing, etc.

Effects of Ozone on Animals. Ozone is a strong pulmonary irritant of the mucous membranes of animals. Even at very low concentrations such as are commonly found in community photochemical air pollution it augments the morbidity effects of respiratory infection and shortens the life span of test animals exposed to both respiratory infection and ozone. At high ozone levels such as are found in certain occupational exposures, ozone causes acute lung injury in laboratory animals characterized by pulmonary congestion and edema; while at still higher concentrations, hemorrhage and death occur.

Recent findings indicate that ozone may also produce secondary systemic effects on body metabolism and function. In addition, radiomimetic effects, where ozone simulates the effects of x-irradiation causing such effects as structural damage to myocardial tissue, increased rate in development of lung adenomas and aging effects have been reported particularly in prolonged exposures.

yet work in a slightly over-ozonated atmosphere, have life spans 7 years shorter than the average among all physicians.[18]

Robert Fettner, experimenting in England with fish exposed to water ozonated eight parts per million, ozone in oxygen, found that fish, living in said ozonated water, experience a sharp decline in longevity, a decline which can be described by a transient decay curve. He further concluded:

> This investigation has demonstrated that exposure to ozone is capable of producing chromatid breakages in human cell cultures, which are apparently identical to those produced by x-rays.[19]

The decline of the life spans or the decline of longevity in man after the flood is also described by a transient decay curve whether by coincidence or not, as is illustrated in Figure 6.

In the pre-flood world there was either no ozone at the surface of the earth, where man and animals breathe, or else it existed in dilutions of parts per trillion, as contrasted with the current atmosphere, where toxic, corrosive ozone exists in parts per hundred million naturally, and higher in some industrialized environments.

The pre-flood world had the better of both ozone potentials.

(1) The ionospheric ozone canopy was thicker, and more efficient at shielding the earth from short wave radiation, especially within the ultra-violet range. Simultaneously it allowed the nonharmful longer wave radiation to pass through.

(2) There was less ozone in the troposphere due to the heat equilibrium, the antediluvian canopy, and the totality of the Greenhouse Effect.

(3) There was greater concentration of water vapor in the lower atmosphere.

(4) There was a greater concentration of carbon dioxide in the entire atmosphere.

---

[18]The number of molecules per cubic centimeter is 2.69×10^{19}. Minimum concentrations of ozone in the free atmosphere are 1 part per 100,000,000, and are somewhat higher naturally, and much higher in some industrialized areas. For instance symptoms of ozone toxicity are common in stratocruisers, submarines, and around arc welding areas. Ozone is a factor in industrial smog. This means that in the atmosphere which we currently breathe, there are a minimum of 2.69×10^{11} molecules of ozone per cubic centimeter, even at this dilution.

Again, we contend that in the pre-flood atmosphere, the concentration of molecules of ozone per cubic centimeter was virtually nil.

[19]Fettner, Robert, *Nature*, London; May 1962, Vol. 194, p. 793.

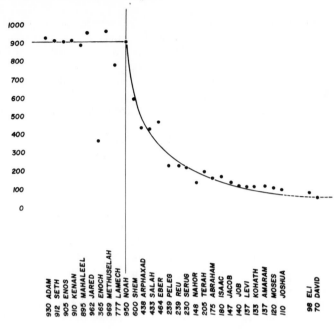

CURVE OF DECLINING LONGEVITY

ANTE-DILUVIAN AND POST-DILUVIAN PATRIARCHS

FIGURE 6

Hence, the fauna (animals) had the best of both possibilities (a better high level ozone shield and a non-ozonated lower atmosphere). Similarly, plants had the better of both potentials, having more water and (in a dew regime) more carbon dioxide both available. We are not suggesting that barley grew nine inches in seven days in the pre-flood world, as has been achieved under experimental conditions. But we do propose that vegetation flourished more than today, and on a pole-to-pole basis.

We further propose that in the pre-flood atmosphere, not only did animals tend to grow larger — we propose that they matured more slowly, and aged much more slowly. Today the average person may inhale ten million times per year, and may inhale the equivalent of one third of a breath of pure ozone. It is proposed that in the pre-flood atmosphere man would not inhale a tenth of a pure breath of ozone in a thousand years, or should we say, in the Methuselaic 969 years.

If mankind lived in an atmosphere of several parts per 10,000 cyanogen or mustard gas, he would display much concern. Research into the physiological effects of ozone is mostly a phenomenon of the last five years. Mankind does live in a mildly corrosive, poisoned, or ozonated atmosphere, and yet is hardly aware of its significance, partly because of the extreme dilution.

Adam and Methuselah lived in a non-ozonated atmosphere. They lived in an era when lizards forgot to quit growing, and dinosaurs abounded. Insects developed 20- and 30-inch wing spans. Birds developed 15- and 25-foot wing spans. Large fish existed. Five-foot frogs and 12-foot turtles were normal. Sloths of 10,000 pounds existed. Mammoths were twice as large in terms of weight as are modern pachyderms. This same principle runs throughout the mammalian world, be it canines and sabertoothed mesonyxes (about as large as Great Danes), be it felines such as sabertoothed panthers and tigers, be it mammoths whose tusks sometimes arched in 300° of a complete circle, or be it man who may have been nine feet tall and 900 years old. "And there were giants in the earth in those days" (Genesis 6:4a).

It may be of interest to mathematicians to discover that after the flood catastrophe one might double the number of generations from Noah, and he can pretty much half the life span. This proceeded down to approximately 1,000 B.C. where the curve finally levelled out at threescore and ten. We suspect that the effects of an ozonated atmosphere, reinforced by a higher level of ultra-violet radiation, produced cumulative effects within the human race. Since the first six generations all died about the same time, could this indicate that the germ tissue, the gametes, were physiologically brought into a new and harsher physical environment?

We further suspect that, with mankind, he became increasingly alarmed when Arphaxad lived 438 years, whereas, great-grandson Peleg lived only 239. Peleg's great-grandson, Nahor, lived but 148. What was happening? How concerned and dismayed must have been those sixth and eighth generation postdiluvians. We suspect here is the basis for the cult of the dead motif, the death psychosis, which so deeply pervaded ancient Egyptian culture where the death of the head of a family became a super-tragic event, and death-journeys up the Nile to mummified entombment became national spectaculars. This is part of ancient thoughts and values.

But evolutionary-uniformitarianism tells us that man has changed for the better and we have little of importance to learn from the past. For creationists and catastrophists, however, this article is an opening wedge into the consideration of the Greenhouse Effect, and paleoclimatology, one part of the far larger subject of the flood-ice catastrophe. This article is a beginning probe, hopefully, to more thorough and comprehensive investigations of the past. Perhaps it is a spur to investigate what would occur in laboratory conditions to animals subjected, not to super-ozonated conditions as in the works of Fettner and Jaffe, *et al,* but rather to completely non-ozonated conditions. Would longevity again become, to some degree, re-established? Would a prevailing gigantism among animals again recur? We suspect so.

Part VII

Conclusions

The following conclusions are made concerning the Greenhouse Effect, and its component, the pre-flood canopy in the troposphere:

1. The ignoring of Genesis and Job by evolutionary-uniformitarians helps neither history nor science.
2. Ancient non-Hebrew traditions of longevity contain cores of truth.
3. Ancient non-Hebrew traditions of a low-lying permanent cloud canopy also contain cores of truth.
4. Animals and, very possibly, man also grew larger in the pre-flood era.
5. Man and, very possibly, animals also lived longer in the pre-flood era.
6. Carbon-14 dating, when integrated within a catastrophic framework, results in one more verification of Biblical chronology, as it has been in other areas, with Biblical archaeology.
7. Catastrophism may have been rejected by evolutionary uniformitarians, but it has hardly been refuted.
8. Popular geology needs to abandon its uniformitarian prejudice.
9. Theologians need to recognize their great lack of cosmological thought.
10. A totally integrated picture, or system, of the flood catastrophe is essential to an understanding of earth history.
11. "A century of uniformitarian thought has set back real progress and knowledge incalculably. Now, with relief, we note that leaders of scientific thought are beginning to express their doubts out loud."[20]
12. The Fear of the Lord is the beginning of wisdom, but fools despise the Lord's wisdom and instruction.

---

[20]Wilson, Talmage, frontpiece, as quoted in Patten, Donald W., *The Biblical Flood and the Ice Epoch, op. cit.*

Carbon-14 Dating of Fossils

Donald E. Chittick

DONALD E. CHITTICK

Dr. Chittick is a native of Salem, Oregon. He received a B.S. in chemistry from Willamette University, and an M.S. and Ph.D. in theoretical chemistry (physical chemistry) was received from Oregon State University. He was on the faculty of the University of Puget Sound, 1960-1968, and is currently visiting professor in chemistry at George Fox College.

Dr. Chittick is listed in *American Men of Science*, and has memberships in the American Chemical Society, the American Association for the Advancement of Science, and the Creation Research Society.

II

CARBON-14 DATING OF FOSSILS

In addition to being interesting objects of study for their own sake, fossils provide very tangible evidence of events of the past. This evidence can be used to supplement other historical data in providing a more detailed account and framework of earth history.

Fossils occur in such a wide variety of types and locations that it will be necessary to limit this discussion to the interesting problem of assigning dates to representative fossil data.

As in other areas of study, data of interest to a paleontologist are explained by fitting them into some type of theoretical framework. This framework is composed of a set of postulates or premises from which certain conclusions regarding the meaning of raw data (fossils in this case) may be drawn by means of deductive logic.

It is possible to draw very different conclusions about some particular data or even all of the data if different starting premises are used. This is a very important point which is often overlooked. What this means is that conclusions regarding the interpretation of paleontological data are ultimately based on faith. Although this may seem surprising, it is true because of the way deductive processes work.

Conclusions drawn using deductive logic can be only as valid as the original premises. These premises are held on faith. Therefore, in discussing any conclusions in his field, a paleontologist in fairness can only say, "I *believe* this data means. . . ." In order to be consistent one attempts to select those premises which are in agreement with his total world view.

Those who accept the Bible as the Word of God revealed to man have a very different world view from those who do not. It is inevitable, therefore, that data from paleontology will mean different things in each view. One may well ask at this point which of the various views is correct. The way one answers this question may vary considerably from individual to individual. For many, however, that view is favored which explains the most data in the simplest manner and with the fewest secondary or additional assumptions.

The issue of dating of fossils is thus a very pertinent one.

First, it is pertinent because of the extreme contrast in the conclusions regarding ages of fossils provided by the Biblical view of history and non-Biblical ones. This contrast should make it easier to come to a decision sooner regarding the validity of one view or another for those who are yet uncommitted.

Secondly, those who hold a Biblical world view have been extensively challenged as to why they continue to believe this view when as is commonly supposed "studies in modern science (fossils for example) have shown this view to be questionable or wrong altogether." Intellectual honesty requires that this challenge be considered by both sides since it is a two-way challenge. In other words, the Biblical position challenges the non-Biblical ones and vice versa.

It may be well to comment briefly on what is meant here by the term Biblical world view. The Biblical world view provides a consistent unified system. To quote Schaeffer,

> . . . everything in the Biblical system goes back to God. I love the Biblical system as a system. While we may not like the connotation of the word *system*, because it sounds rather cold, this does not mean that Biblical teaching is not a system. Everything goes back to the beginning and thus the system has a unique beauty and perfection because everything is under the apex of the system. Everything begins with the kind of God who is "there." This is the beginning and apex of the whole, and everything flows from this in a non-contradictory way. The Bible says God is a living God and it tells us much about Him, but, most significantly perhaps, for twentieth century man, it speaks of Him as both a personal God and an infinite God. . . . This personal-infinite God of the Bible is the Creator of all else. God created all things, and He created them out of nothing. Therefore, everything else is finite, everything else is the creature. He alone is the infinite Creator.[1]

According to the Bible, history began at Creation.

A comment on Biblical creation may help to clear up some possible questions at this point. To quote one scientist who believes in Biblical creation,

> Does the Bible establish a date, as well as a method? In a specific sense it does not; but in a general sense it most assuredly does. The general *method* is fiat creation — perfect natural order brought out of nothing by the Word of a sovereign God. The

---

[1]Schaeffer, Francis A., *Escape from Reason*, Inter-Varsity Press, Chicago, Illinois, 1968.

general *time* is clearly at the creation of the first man and woman; a time delineated with sufficient clarity (Gen. 5 and 11 are not just casual genealogies!) that we can establish it about 5,000 B.C., yet also with sufficient obscurity that it is not merely an adding machine problem as Ussher seemed to think.[2]

A discussion, therefore, of the topic of dating fossils is justified for at least two reasons. First, one must evaluate and examine new data in order to meet the challenge to remain intellectually honest. Second, Biblical creation is a very powerful tool for interpreting the fossil data. It allows the data to be integrated into a unified and consistent whole. This provides a firm base for further scientific research and is an aid to the science of paleontology.

Many methods for dating of fossils have been proposed. Some of these are limited to relative dates. They establish only that a particular fossil is either older or younger than some other fossil. No attempt is made to assign a historical date in years. Other methods seek to establish an absolute date in terms of years. Most commonly, Biblical and non-Biblical views are more concerned with absolute dating methods. Of these one of the most widely employed and discussed is the carbon-14 technique.

Before discussing the results of carbon-14 (abbreviated C-14) dating, a brief review of some of the principles involved may be useful. Carbon-14 is a radioactive variety of the element carbon. C-14 atoms are slightly more massive or heavier than ordinary atoms of carbon, having a relative mass of 14 as compared with 12. C-14 is the designation of this heavier type of carbon atom.

C-14 atoms are radioactive while ordinary carbon-12 atoms are not, although the two types of carbon behave the same chemically. While ordinary carbon and C-14 react chemically in the same way, the presence of C-14 can be detected by its radioactivity. It is this radioactivity that also allows the possibility of using C-14 as a clock for telling the age of fossils. C-14 dating, therefore, is one of the radioactive dating methods and follows many of the same principles as other radioactive dating methods. These principles are reviewed in my chapter on the age of the earth.

C-14 is of special interest in the dating of organic fossil remains because carbon is the central constituent of all organic matter. This allows for the dating of the fossil organic matter directly rather than being limited to dating by association with surrounding rocks or other sedimentary material.

---

[2]Whitelaw, Robert L., "Radiocarbon Confirms Biblical Creation (And So Does Potassium – Argon)" *Creation Research Society Quarterly*, vol. 5, number 2, September 1968.

Let us briefly outline the process by which C-14 is incorporated into organic remains and the basis of using it as a method of dating. Carbon found in the biosphere or the carbon cycle of nature is composed almost entirely of atoms of the C-12 variety which are not radioactive. However, in the upper atmosphere molecules of nitrogen gas which compose nearly 80 per cent of the gasses of the atmosphere, are being continually bombarded by cosmic rays which results in a transmutation into C-14. Eventually these new C-14 atoms unite chemically with oxygen in the upper atmosphere to become carbon dioxide which, after circulation to surface regions, is then incorporated into plants by means of photosynthesis. Animals, too, have C-14 in their bodies as a result of eating plants containing it.

When a plant or animal dies, the organism ceases to take in new C-14 atoms and those it already has will slowly decay away because of their radioactivity. The longer the plant or animal has been dead, the less C-14 it will possess in any of its carbon-containing remains. In principle, then by knowing the amount of C-14 the animal or plant had at death, the mount of C-14 remaining now, and the rate of decay of C-14, it should be possible to calculate the amount of time since death. In other words, it may be possible to date the fossil.

A C-14 age for a fossil obtained by a calculation of this type will be only as accurate or reliable as the information on which the calculation is based. First, we shall briefly examine the nature of this information and then some of the results of C-14 dating.

After obtaining a suitable sample, which is sometimes a considerable problem in itself, a determination of the present amount of C-14 it contains is made. Next, the rate at which C-14 decays with time must be known. This rate for radioactive processes is expressed as the half-life and has a value of 5,568 years as used in most C-14 dating work. This is used rather than the more recent and accurate value of 5,730 years in order to avoid confusion in comparing recent determinations with the many older ones when 5,568 was generally accepted. (However, it is a relatively simple matter to convert dates based on the 5,568-year half-life value to the more accurate 5,730 one. All that is necessary is a simple multiplication by 1.03.) The half-life of C-14, or the rate of C-14 decay, seems to be fairly reliable and does not seem to cause much problem in the dating calculation.

Most discussions on the accuracy and reliability of C-14 dates concern themselves with the remaining item of information which enters into an age calculation. That item is the amount of C-14 present in the animal or plant when it died. One must either make an assumption as to what this amount was, or one must have an object whose age has been accurately and independently determined by some other means.

When dating by C-14 first began to be used, two assumptions were made. The first assumption was that the earth was extremely old in accord with the non-creation, or uniformitarian, position. This led to the second assumption. Since the earth was supposedly billions of years old, the rate of C-14 production in the atmosphere and the rate of C-14 decay would long ago have reached a balance. It has been calculated that the time required to reach this balance is only about 30,000 years.[3] Hence, if the earth is billions of years old, C-14 should long ago have built up to a constant amount and remained there. In other words, it was assumed that the amount of C-14 in the biosphere when most fossils were still living was this constant amount, generally accepted now to be about 18.4 disintegrations per minute per gram of plant or animal carbon.

The assumption that the rate of formation and the rate of decay are an equilbrium allows the use of the "equilibrium" C-14 as the amount of this radioactive substance present at death of a fossil. Calculation of an age for a fossil on this basis is then a fairly simple matter. For example, a fossil whose C-14 content was one-half the equilibrium value would be 5,568 years old, which is the value for the half-life of C-14. The smaller the amount of C-14 remaining in a fossil, the older it would be concluded to be on the basis of this assumption.

C-14 would be a very effective and relatively simple dating method if the assumption of the constancy of C-14 in the atmosphere of the past were to be true. Scientists working with carbon dating have, therefore, attempted to check the validity of this assumption. For example, W. F. Libby, who won the Nobel Prize for his work on C-14 dating, has discussed this point, along with the general validity of C-14 as a dating tool. After comparing C-14 dates with a summary of historical data such as Egyptology and tree ring dates, he continues with a discussion of the assumption of constancy of C-14 in the biosphere. Dr. Libby states,

> The radiocarbon content of the biosphere depends on three supposedly independent geophysical quantities:
>
> (1) the average cosmic ray intensity over a period of 8,000 years (the average life of radiocarbon) as measured in our solar system but outside the earth's magnetic field;

---

[3]Cook, Melvin A., "Radiological Dating and Some Pertinent Applications of Historical Interest, Do Radiological 'Clocks' Need Repair," *Creation Research Society Quarterly*, Vol. 5, No. 2, Sept. 1968, p. 69.

(2) the magnitude (but not the orientation, because of the
relatively rapid mixing over the earth's surface) of the magnetic field in the vicinity of the earth, averaged over the
same period; and

(3) the degree of mixing of the oceans during the same period.
The question of the accuracy of radiocarbon dates, therefore, is of interest to geophysics in general, as well as archae-
ologists, geologists, and historians who use the dates.[4]

In concluding the discussion Dr. Libby states his reasons for
believing in the constancy of the cosmic ray flux and in the probable
constancy of the mixing of the oceans. Then he goes on to say,

The question of the constancy of the magnetic field near the earth
and its effect on the rate of production of carbon-14 is almost
completely open.

His conclusion is that the magnetic field,

. . . has probably remained constant to within the indicated limits
of 10 to 20 per cent over the past 4,000 or 5,000 years. . . .[5]

In other words, it seems quite risky to push radiocarbon dates back
past about 5,000 years ago, even with the equilibrium model.

In discussing the historical data Dr. Libby states that C-14 and
historical dates agree quite well back to about 5,000 years ago.
While discussing plots of the historical data he states,

These plots (i.e., historical dates vs. the uncertainty in the dates)
of the data suggest that the Egyptian historical dates beyond 4,000
years ago may be somewhat too old, perhaps 5 centuries too old
at 5,000 years ago, with decrease in the error to 0 at 4,000 years
ago. In this connection it is noteworthy that the earliest astronomical fix is at 4,000 years ago, that all older dates have errors, and
that these errors are more or less cumulative with time before
4,000 years ago.[6]

In passing it is interesting to note that if the mixing of the oceans
has a bearing on the reliability of radiocarbon dates, then a consideration of a global event like the Genesis flood would be of
considerable importance.

More recent work than that of the article by Dr. Libby quoted

---

[4]Libby, W. F., "Accuracy of Radiocarbon Dates," *Science*, Vol. 140,
April 19, 1963, p. 278-280.
[5]*Op. cit.* p. 280.
[6]*Op. cit.* p. 278.

above has shown that the assumption of a constant rate of C-14 production is not valid. For example, Geochron Laboratories, Inc., reports,

> Perhaps the most important single assumption of the radiocarbon dating method is that the rate of C-14 production by cosmic rays in the upper atmosphere has been constant. This is a difficult assumption to verify (or to disprove). If the rate of C-14 production has varied, then so has the level of C-14 activity in the atmosphere, hydrosphere, and biosphere. A radiocarbon date is computed assuming that the level of C-14 activity at the time of isolation (or death) of the sample is known (i.e., constant). The age of the sample is the time necessary for the assumed initial activity to have decreased to the present measured activity by a known rate, the half-life.
>
> Working the problem backwards, investigators have measured the activity of samples of known age and have computed the initial activity these samples must have had at the time of isolation from the C-14 reservoir. It has been shown on the basis of these investigations that variations from the assumed initial activity of some of these samples do exist. Recent elaborate studies have now demonstrated conclusively that the initial activity of C-14 samples and thus the rate of C-14 production has varied with time. Most recently, the work of Suess (1965, J. Geophys. Res. V 70, p. 5937-5952) has clearly pointed out these variations.[7]

As mentioned earlier, finding a good fossil sample to use for carbon dating is also somewhat of a problem. In another article by Dr. Libby and co-workers, this problem is evaluated. The article states,

> Until recently, the radiocarbon dating of archaeological bone samples was based primarily on the dating of associated charcoal, and in some cases on the natural calcium carbonate contents of bones. However, dates by correlation with charcoal may not always be correct. Even greater doubt exists on the accuracy of dates based on calcium carbonate which may have been replaced by groundwater carbonate of varying age.[8]

The article then describes a more direct method:

> It is now possible to date bones directly from their content of or-

[7]Libby, W. F., "On the Accuracy of Radiocarbon (C-14) Dates," *The Geochronicle*, Geochron Laboratories, Inc., Vol. 2, No. 2, June, 1966, p. 1.

[8]Berger, Rainer: Amos G. Harney; and W. F. Libby, "Radiocarbon Dating of Bone and Shell from Their Organic Components," *Science*, Vol. 144, p. 999-1001, May 22, 1964.

ganic carbon or collagen. There is no known natural mechanism by which collagen may be altered to yield a false age.[9]

There has been some confusion among laymen concerning carbon dating of fossil bones. Bones are composed primarily of calcium minerals and if they are very old, do not usually contain any organic carbon. Organic carbon is necessary for carbon dating. This is the reason why a more direct method of dating bones by searching for remaining organic matter was sought. Even with the collagen method, however, there are difficulties. Libby's article continues,

> However, the collagen content of bones decreases with age to such low concentrations that isolation of sufficient collagen for radiocarbon dating becomes difficult with the oldest bones. The oldest specimen that had been dated in this way had a collagen content of about 0.16 per cent. It was about 9,000 years old (UCLA-630).[10]

By way of summary one can see that the radiocarbon method of dating is not quite the simple matter that it might at first glance appear to be. In the first place, as Dr. Libby and others have pointed out, the method is dependent on a number of assumptions, some of which are highly questionable. For example, one of the main assumptions, the C-14 content of the atmosphere during the past, has not been established and is very open to question.

In addition to this difficulty, the method disagrees with accepted historical dates before about 2,000 B.C. Thus, while a certain sample of organic remains will yield on analysis a particular amount of C-14, the problem is to interpret this data into a reliable date. It is fairly easy to obtain agreement concerning the remaining amount of C-14 in a sample, but what assumptions should be used to interpret this data? Again, I would like to suggest that two approaches to making these assumptions are available:

(1) assumptions made in a Biblical framework of Special Creation, and
(2) assumptions made in a non-Biblical framework.

Probably the majority of published works on C-14 dating has been within a world view in which the Bible is not considered as a reliable historical document. *Catastrophism has not been consid-*

---

[9]*Ibid.*, p. 999.
[10]*Ibid.*

ered. This results in the C-14 data being interpreted by means of those assumptions which are consistent with the uniformitarian (non-catastrophic) view. Suppose, however, that one were to interpret the C-14 data within a world view in which the Bible is considered to be a reliable historical document. What effect would assumptions consistent with this view have on conclusions regarding C-14 data?

As mentioned before, one of the necessary items of information needed to make a calculation of age is the amount of C-14 in the atmosphere while a fossil was still alive. Since we have no direct knowledge of this amount, we are left with the necessity of making an assumption as to what it was. Using the Bible as a guide, everything began at Creation about 7,000 years ago. Assuming the rate of production of C-14 to have been roughly the same then as now, it can be calculated that it would take approximately 30,000 years for the rate of production of C-14 and the rate of decay to become equal. When these rates become equal, the amount of C-14 in the atmosphere (or biosphere) would remain constant. A conclusion to be drawn from this is that in the time available since Creation, C-14 could not have reached equilibrium where the two rates are equal. This means that C-14 should still be forming faster than it is decaying. Now let us compare this conclusion with the actually measured data to see if the two are in agreement. If they are, this would lend support to correctness of our original assumption that the Bible is accurate historically.

Cook points out that work by Libby, Hess, Lingenfelter, and Suess has shown that the rate of formation is indeed faster than the rate of decay.[11] The rate of decay is only about 70 per cent of the rate of formation. Although the fact that the rate of decay is still less than the rate of formation is well established, various explanations are offered by those who wish to avoid the direct implications of this situation. The direct implication is that the atmosphere has an age considerably less than 30,000 years. Also, a condition of non-equilibrium for C-14 is in agreement with other radioactive data which indicate a young earth as discussed in the chapter on the age of the earth.[12]

There are further interesting assumptions one might make which could have a bearing on how the C-14 evidence is interpreted. If we consider the implications of a world-wide flood as described in the Book of Genesis and the probable conditions which existed before this event, several things suggest themselves. First, the

---

[11]Cook, *loc. cit.*, p. 69.
[12]See next chapter.

fossil record indicates a much more luxurious growth of vegetation covering the earth in pre-flood times. The great reserves of fossil fuels such as coal and oil, and the limestone beds indicate a biosphere which was many times richer in carbon than it is today. This fact and the consideration that the flood occurred much closer in time to the start of the build-up of C-14 would lead to the conclusion that the percentage of C-14 in the pre-flood biosphere was very much less than now.

This would have the effect that fossils from that time, the fossil fuels and limestones, would have very little, if any, C-14 left. Limestones and fossil fuels do, in fact, have virtually no C-14 activity. Fossils formed by the flood would also have very little C-14 left. If these fossils were dated using a non-Biblical view, however, they would be dated as very, very old, so that there would have been enough time to allow the assumed high C-14 to decay almost to zero. Thus most fossils dated by C-14, if they have actual dates older than about 2500 B.C., are assigned calendar dates either at or about the time of the flood or, are assigned dates in many thousands of years. Which assignment will be made is determined primarily by the assumptions made concerning the amount of C-14 in the biosphere in ancient times, both before and after the flood. The nature of these assumptions are, in turn, determined by the world view of the investigator. Assumptions consistent with a Biblical world view are not in conflict with known facts of C-14 data and have the added advantage that they lead to predicted results which are in general agreement with observed facts.

Those who have used the Bible as a guide in investigating archaeological and other historical remains have found it to be entirely reliable. Indications are that this will continue to be the case as more sophisticated tools such as C-14 are made available to the historians.

> All Scripture is inspired by God and is useful for teaching the faith and correcting error, for resetting the direction of a man's life, and training him in good living. The Scriptures are the comprehensive equipment of the man of God, and fit him fully *for all branches of his work* (II Timothy 3:15 Phillips).

Dating the Earth and Fossils

Donald E. Chittick

III

DATING THE EARTH AND FOSSILS

The concept of a *time scale* as it relates to the history of the earth and the life upon it is of interest to us for a very much more important reason than just to satisfy curiosity or to serve as a topic for a stimulating discussion. It is a relevant question not only because truth and knowledge are important, but because time is intimately associated with a very basic philosophical issue. The issue of Special Creation as opposed to a naturalistic approach to the question of origins is closely associated with the evaluation of a time scale.

As used here, the term Special Creation refers to the idea that events described in the first few chapters of the book of Genesis actually happened in space and time. In this view, direct acts of God resulted in a full-blown creation complete in all details necessary for life as described in Genesis. This view holds that chemical and physical laws, however complete our knowledge of them may be, will never be sufficient to explain or account for their own origin or existence, or the existence of the universe.

The naturalistic approach, on the other hand, attempts to explain the present state of the universe by starting with some postulated primitive conditions, matter, energy, and natural laws, and allowing these to interact in some way to arrive at the present state. The naturalistic approach has as one of its basic tenets the absence of any supernaturalism. Its tenet is chance.

The naturalistic approach requires a time scale for the earth and its life which is very very great as we normally think of time. Current thinking in this framework considers the earth to be several billions of years old, usually around 4.5 billion, or more, and life on earth to have been here for approximately 2 billion years. How is this vast amount of time arrived at? Are such figures required by the available data? And are they made more certain by recent investigations and clocking methods? In this chapter we will discuss these "geochronological" questions.

The amount of time the earth has been in existence has been central to the debate between Special Creation and naturalism. Using several lines of evidence, geneological tables among them, the Special Creation position arrives at an age for the earth measured in thousands of years. Naturalism, on the other hand,

57

claims very much more time was involved, and, furthermore, it claims that the data of science support this conclusion.

The issue has been needlessly confused by various attempts and schemes for "harmonizing" the two views. One of these schemes for harmonizing Special Creation with naturalism was the so-called "Gap Theory" or "Ruin-Reconstruction Theory" which became quite widely espoused among some Special Creationists. The Gap Theory postulated as much time as needed by naturalism but this time was inserted between Genesis 1:1 and 1:2. It is not our purpose to discuss these schemes here except to point out that all failed to a greater or lesser degree to harmonize naturalism and Special Creation. While ages for the earth might be to some extent harmonized in this way, ages of fossils, and especially fossil men, continued to present problems.

The purpose of this chapter will be to consider two questions. First, what is the basis for the prevalent view of time in vast amounts for the history of the earth and life on it? Second, what are some of the pertinent and recent facts which may assist in evaluating a time scale?

Naturalistic Time Scale

In seeking the basis for the time scale used by advocates of a naturalistic approach, one may consider what the naturalists themselves say about its origin and basis. Weisz, for example, states:

> By this time (i.e., Pasteur's) the alternative to special creation, namely, the idea of continuity and historical succession, or EVOLUTION, had occurred to a number of thinkers. Some of these recognized that any concept of evolution demanded an earth of sufficiently great age, and they set out to estimate this age. Newton's law of gravitation provided the tool with which to calculate the weight of the earth. One could then bring a small weighed ball of earth to white heat and measure its rate of cooling. From such measurements, one could calculate how long it must have taken the whole earth to cool to its present state. This provided the many millions of years required to fit evolution into, and this time span gradually lengthened as techniques of clocking improved.[1]

Weisz seems to be saying that the idea of an old earth is a logical corollary to a philosophical position. In other words, it arises as a philosophical necessity if Special Creation is rejected

---

[1]Paul B. Weisz: *The Science of Biology* (New York, McGraw-Hill Book Company, 1959), p. 636.

and not necessarily from factual observation. He implies further that techniques of clocking support this and have caused this time scale to be lengthened. We shall have more to say about clocking techniques later.

Simpson, *et al,* (Biologists), in a section headed, "Time and the Earth," state:

> History is what happens through a span of time. To follow it we need first of all a time scale on which to orient its events. Where should our scale start? Was there a beginning of time? That is a question that science cannot possibly answer. It is difficult, perhaps impossible, to imagine literally infinite time, but the problem must be left to religion or philosophy.[2]

Again one's choice of time scale is seen to be basically a religious or philosophical question.

Granted then that the choice of a time scale is a religious or philosophical one, rather than one demanded by clocking facts, why does the anti-supernaturalistic (or naturalistic) approach require such a vast amount of time compared to Special Creation? Wald, who apparently rejects Special Creation, has summarized the argument rather succinctly. He writes:

> To make an organism demands the right substances in the right proportions and in the right arrangement. We do not think that anything more is needed — *but that is problem enough.*
>
> One has only to contemplate the magnitude of this task to concede that the spontaneous generation of living organism is impossible. Yet here we are — as a result, I believe, of spontaneous generation. . . .[3]

Wald then explains what he means by an impossibility. He means that by using the method of chance, it is an event of extremely low probability. This is how the time element comes in. He continues:

> In such a problem as the spontaneous origin of life we have no way of assessing probabilities beforehand, or even of deciding what we mean by trial. The origin of a living organism is undoubtedly a step-wise phenomenon, each step with its own probability and its own conditions of trial. Of one thing we can be sure, however:

[2]G. G. Simpson, C. S. Pittendrigh, L. H. Tiffany: *Life — An Introduction to Biology* (New York, Harcourt, Brace and Co., 1957), p. 734.

[3]G. Wald: *Physics and Chemistry of Life* (New York, A Scientific American Book, 1955), p. 8 ff.

whatever constitutes a trial, *more such trials occur the longer the interval of time.* (emphasis mine)

The important point is that since the origin of life belongs in the category of at-least-once phenomena, time is on its side. However improbable we regard this event, or any of the steps which it involves, *given enough time,* it will almost certainly happen at least once. And for life as we know it, with its capacity for growth and reproduction, once may be enough.

Time is the hero of the plot. The time with which we have to deal is of the order of two billion years. *What we regard as impossible on the basis of human experience is meaningless here.* Given so much time, the "impossible" becomes possible, the possible probable, and the probable virtually certain. One has only to wait: *time itself performs the miracles.* (emphasis mine)

Vast amounts of time for the history of the earth is a concept arising from a naturalistic philosophy. It arises as a philosophical requirement when Special Creation is rejected. It is not, as is commonly supposed, a result of factual observations.

At first glance, the logic leading to the conclusion of great time spans seems plausible enough. A second and closer look, however, reveals that it fails to consider several important points. Naturalistic philosophy fails to show why Special Creation should be rejected or why it is not true. It would also seem that to reject Special Creation in favor of chance (naturalism), one must relinquish any means of testing the truth of further conclusions. In other words, if human experience (or the world of observable facts) is not to be trusted, what is?

Montgomery has discussed this point:

This "Verifiability Criterion of Meaning" arose from the discovery (set forth by Whitehead and Russell in the *Principia*) that assertions in mathematics and deductive logic are tautologous, i.e., they state nothing factual about the world, but follow from the a priori assumptions of the deductive system. Such "analytic" sentences can be verified without recourse to the world of fact, since they say nothing about the world; but other assertions (nontautological, or "synthetic" affirmations) must be tested by the data of the real world if we are to discover their truth or falsity.

Thus any proposition, upon inspection, will fall into one of the following categories: (1) Analytic sentences, which are true or false solely by virtue of their logical form, *ex hypothesi.* Such assertions, though essential to thought and potentially meaningful, are often termed "trivial," since they never provide information about the world of experience. Example: "All husbands are married," whose truth follows entirely from the definition of the word "husband." (2) Synthetic sentences, which are true or false according to the application of the Verifiability Criterion set forth above. Such sentences are sometimes termed "informative," because they do potentially give information about the world. Example: "Jesus died at Jerusalem," which can be tested through an examination of historical evidence. (3) Meaningless sentences, embracing all affirmations which are neither analytic nor synthetic. Such sentences are incapable of testing, for they neither express tautological judgments (they are not statements whose truth depends on their logical form) nor do they affirm anything about the real world which is testable by investigating the world. Example: the philosopher F. L. Bradley's claim that "the Absolute enters into, but is itself incapable of, evolution and progress." Such a statement is clearly not tautologous, for it is not deduced from a prioris of logic, nor is it capable of any test which could conceivably determine its truth or falsity. Thus it is meaningless or nonsensical (in the technical meaning of "nonsense," i.e., without verifiable sense).[4]

As quoted previously, Wald stated:

What we regard as impossible on the basis of human experience (i.e., the spontaneous generation of life) is meaningless here.

In effect, Wald seems to be saying that by any basis of test or comparison with the real world, spontaneous generation is invalid and so it is necessary to postulate its truth somewhere outside human experience. Thus, the assertions of spontaneous generation of life and the associated vast amounts of time are meaningless in the sense of analytical philosophy. The truth or falsity of such an assertion is not capable of being tested in the realm of human experience or the real world.

A second point which arises concerning naturalistic thinking involves making the extremely improbable become probable by having many, many chances take place. It would seem that in the usual way of regarding probability, (i.e., the more chances involved where each chance is less than one) the longer time, the *less* probable an event becomes, not *more* probable.

For example, suppose a single event has a 50-50 chance of occurring, that is, it has a chance of one-half. Suppose a second event also has a 50-50 chance of occurring. If the two events must be connected in order to give a particular outcome, the chance of the outcome is $\frac{1}{2} \times \frac{1}{2}$, or $\frac{1}{4}$, which is smaller than either single

---

[4]John W. Montgomery: *Crisis in Lutheran Theology* (Grand Rapids, Michigan, Baker Book House, 1967), p. 26.

event alone. Thus, the more such connected events the smaller becomes the chance of the final outcome.

Entropy

A third point which seems to be commonly overlooked is the physical basis for time. Eddington has suggested that the second law of thermodynamics is the physical basis of time. The second law is a statement of the observation that the amount of order in a system constantly decreases. Given two connected events, the one with the greater order occurred first in time. The universe is going toward a more disordered state. This is usually expressed as the law of entropy. Entropy always increases. Local temporary fluctuations of entropy may occur, but they will not accumulate.

Maruyama has discussed this point from several angles in connection with questions relating to the theory of organic evolution. He writes:

> The seventh logical level (of the second law of thermodynamics) is that it is highly unlikely that random changes accumulate systematically and monotonically into one direction. A corollary of this consideration is that independent random changes tend to destroy structure: if a structure is built at all, it has to be built by a sudden change rather than by a gradual and monotonical increase of structuredness. This was the basis of Reichenback's argument that, given a motion picture of an event in which the structuredness gradually changes, there is only one direction the film can be run to make sense.[5]

If this is true, then it would seem that the idea of a gradual increase from disorder to order required by spontaneous generation where time is the "hero of the plot" is in conflict with one of our most fundamental of all physical laws. It is in conflict with what would "make sense." Again, the second law does not say life via chance is impossible, but rather that it is highly improbable. One might ask the question then: "Do men of science seek a probable or an improbable explanation for things?" The answer one would hope for is that dogma arising from a certain set of philosophical presuppositions would not prevent a probable explanation from being considered.

We have considered the first of two aspects involved with dating scales, the origin of the idea of vast amounts of time. We have seen that this idea arises as a result of rejecting Special Creation.

---

[5]M. Maruyama: "A Postscript to the Second Cybernetics" *American Scientist*, vol. 51, No. 3. Autumn 1963, p. 250A-256A.

Clocking Techniques

Let us, therefore, consider now a second feature of the issue. This feature concerns the claim that "clocking" techniques support vast amounts of time. Although there may be questions raised about the nature of the naturalists' time scale from a logic viewpoint, yet it is generally claimed that clocking techniques support it.

For example, Simpson, *et al*, after pointing out that science cannot answer the question of when time started or even if it did start, state that most time scales for the earth begin with the time of origin of the solar system. They then claim that it is known that this was extremely long ago and that clocking techniques assure us of this.

> We know that the solar system is more than 2 billion years old because there are rocks exposed in the earth's crust that are over that age. The dating has been done by study of radioactive minerals.[6]

It is claimed that certain clocking techniques, radioactive ones in this instance, give us knowledge of how old rocks are and, therefore, how old the earth is. On what basis can claims like these be made?

Before examining some of the specific dating techniques, it may be well to review the conditions necessary for reading time on any type of clock. In order to tell time or assign dates using any clock, mechanical, radiological, geological, or whatever, two things must be known. First, one must have a knowledge of the rate at which the clock runs, and second, one must know when the clock started to operate, or in other words, where to set it to zero. Both of these conditions must be met in order to tell time or date an event.

By way of illustration, suppose we consider an ordinary spring-powered mechanical clock. Assume that the large hand is pointing at the numeral 6 and that the small hand is pointing half-way between the numerals two and three. Does this mean that the correct time is now 2:30? Even if we observed that this clock accurately ticked off the minutes and hours, we could still not be certain what time it was by reading this clock. Something more than just an accurate knowledge of the rate at which this clock runs must be known. We must know a second condition: "Was the clock set to international standard time?"

In dating the earth's rocks and fossils it is claimed that the most

---

[6]G. G. Simpson, C. S. Pittendrigh, L. H. Tiffany, *op. cit.*, p. 734.

accurate method is the radioactive technique. As in other methods, two things must be known in this case also, i.e., rate and a zero or beginning of time.

Let us review first the rate question. Radioactive dating is based on the fact that certain naturally occurring elements are radioactive. This means that the atoms which compose these elements decompose into new elements and give off certain radiations and decay products in the process. Analysis of this situation has shown that the rate for the decay process follows an exponential law. This means that in a certain definite amount of time one-half of any given sample will have decayed. This is true regardless of the starting amount.

For example, if the time of half-life for a certain radioactive element is one month and we were to start with, say, thirty-two pounds, at the end of one month sixteen pounds of the original element would remain. The sixteen pounds which decayed would have been transformed into some new element. At the end of two months only one-half of one-half, or eight pounds, of the original element would remain. At the end of three months only four pounds would remain, etc. The time taken for a given sample of a radioactive substance to decay to one-half the original amount is termed the half-life.

Known external physical and chemical conditions do not seem to greatly affect the half-life for any radioactive element. Half-lives are in effect the rate at which the radioactive clock runs and these present rates are known to a fairly high degree of certainty. Let us assume, for the sake of argument, that present rates have not changed during the time the earth has been in existence. We need now to consider a second point.

Calibration of Radioactive Clock

It is on the second clocking requirement, however, where some difficulty arises. This concerns the "setting" of the radioactive clock. In order to do this, one must have knowledge of initial conditions. Without these, it is impossible to tell how long the radioactive clocks have been running. The importance of radioactive dating to concepts of earth history is emphasized by Faul:

> The principles of measuring long periods of elapsed time are outlined in this little book. As long as we stay on Earth, these methods are all based on radioactive decay. . . .[7]

---

[7] Henry Faul: *Ages of Rocks, Planets, and Stars* (New York, McGraw-Hill Book Co., 1966) p. vi.

Since the radioactive clock is widely used in dating and it is supposed to be the most accurate one for measurements of events in the history of the earth, how is knowledge of initial or primordial earth conditions obtained? In other words, how is the radioactive clock set to zero time?

As mentioned earlier, the radioactive decay process causes a particular quantity of an element to become less and less at a rate dependent on its half life. During the decay process, new elements are formed. These are known as decay products. Decay products thus build up and accumulate as the original radioactive material decreases in amount.

In principle then, there are at least two ways which suggest themselves as a means of telling the passage of time using radioactive decay. One would be by measuring the present amount of a radioactive material and comparing it with the original amount when the decay process started, i.e., at zero time. By knowing the rate of decay, the original amount and the amount present now, it should be possible to calculate the amount of time involved since decay started. The problem with this method is in knowing the amount of starting material.

Suppose, for example, that we have a substance with a radioactive half-life of one thousand years (i.e., we know the decay rate.) Suppose further, that the amount of the substance present now is three pounds. If the original amount is assumed to be six pounds, one-half of the original would have decayed. Since the half-life is one thousand years, this would mean that one thousand years had elapsed since decay started. On the other hand, if the original amount is assumed to have been twelve pounds, instead of six, two thousand years would have passed since the decay process started. After one thousand years one-half the original twelve, or six pounds, would remain, and after an additional thousand years one-half of the six pounds, or three pounds (the present amount), would remain. Thus, the amount of time elapsed since the decay process began is dependent not only on the amount now present and the decay rate, but also on the assumed starting amount.

The original amount of material must be known in order to set the radioactive clock to zero. *If the original amount is only set by assumption, the "age" obtained will be only as accurate as the assumption.* We have just seen in this example how two different assumptions about starting amounts led to two different ages.

The second way, in principle, which a radioactive decay process might be used to estimate the passage of time is based on the accumulation of decay products. As radioactive decay proceeds, decay products continue to accumulate. By measuring the amount of decay products and knowing from half-life values the rate at which they accumulate, it should be possible to tell how long the process has been going on.

A similar problem arises with this decay-products method as in the first method, however. In addition to knowing the rate of formation of decay products and the present amount of them, it is also necessary to know the original amount of them before decay started. It is not sufficient just to assume zero amount of material. In most cases the decay products are just like materials already naturally present in the sample even when no radioactive decay has occurred. In other words, we are back to the problem of knowing the original conditions. In the case of the age of the earth, it is obvious that no scientist made records of the initial condition.

Suppose we use an analogy to help illustrate the situation. Like most analogies, it cannot be pushed too far without running into problems, but it may help to make the situation more clear.

Let us choose a burning candle to be similar to an element undergoing radioactive decay. Futher, let us suppose that our candle burns at the rate of one inch every hour. This is analogous to the half-life rate for radioactivity. When we measure the candle we find that it is exactly six inches high (analogous to the present amount of radioactivity.) Now the burning candle is six inches high and disappearing at the rate of one inch every hour. We ask the question, How long has the candle been burning? It is impossible to answer this question unless we know how long the candle was to start with. Starting conditions must be known or we cannot say when zero time was. There is no absolute way of calibrating our "clock."

As in the case of radioactive decay, a burning candle forms "decay" products. Carbon dioxide is formed when the candle burns. But carbon dioxide is also naturally present in the air so that measuring the decay product (carbon dioxide) will hardly help us either in finding how long the candle has been burning. We do not know the amount of CO_2 in the air when the candle started burning. If we make the assumption that all the CO_2 in the atmosphere came from our burning candle, we would arrive at the answer that our candle had been burning for a very long time, indeed!

Estimates of the age of the earth, based on radioactive decay methods, do not give ages independent of certain assumptions. The "ages" so obtained are only as accurate as the assumptions on which they are based. It is my observation that scientists who reject Special Creation make different assumptions from those who accept Special Creation. In the final analysis, dating the earth, even by radioactive methods is a religious issue. As we quoted earlier, Simpson, *et al*, state:

> History is what happens through a span of time. To follow it we need first of all a time scale on which to orient its events. Where should our scale start? Was there a beginning of time? That is a question that science cannot possibly answer. It is difficult, perhaps impossible, to imagine literally infinite time, but the problem must be left to religion or philosophy.[8]

If the age of the earth is deduced from certain assumptions using deductive logic, do we have any guide in making reasonable assumptions other than from philosophical necessity? The answer would appear to be that we do. Science uses both inductive and deductive logic. Deductive logic begins with a set of asumptions and proceeds by the rules of logic to a corresponding set of conclusions. Inductive logic looks at the available data or facts and invents reasonable assumptions for deductive logic to work on. From the facts and the inductive method then, some bounds are set for making reasonable assumptions. In other words, we seek to make assumptions which seem to be in agreement with physical reality.

To return for a moment to our candle illustration. We can see how inductive logic might work in helping us to make reasonable assumptions. The length of time the candle was burning depends on our assumption about the original length of the candle. We are not free to induce the assumption that the candle was one hundred miles high to start with, for example. The physical strength of wax would not support a candle that high. Thus, by the inductive method the relevant facts place certain limits on our assumptions if they are to be reasonable.

How then does the inductive approach help us in the case of making reasonable assumptions for estimating ages using the data from radioactivity? To answer this question, perhaps we can examine several of the well-known methods proposed for radioactive dating.

The phenomenon of radioactivity itself leads us to draw certain boundary conditions as Hurley has pointed out:

> The measurement of time by study of the continuous breakdown of radioactive elements has had great impact on science and philosophy. We have learned that the naturally occurring radio-

---

[8]G. G. Simpson, C. S. Pittendrigh, L. H. Tiffany, *op. cit.*

active elements are constantly decreasing in abundance, and this phenomenon forces upon us a new realization. It demands a creation of these elements, and, therefore, of all elements, at some definite time in the not-too-distant past.[9]

Hurley correctly calls attention to the fact that the elements cannot have been around forever or we would not now have any significant amounts of the decaying ones left. The point is that the elements had a definite starting point in time.

Pleochroic Halos

How long ago and under what conditions did the elements come into existence? Recent investigations concerning pleochroic halos may aid in answering these questions. (Pleochroic halos are minute circular discolorations in sections of rock crystals. These halos are produced by specks of radioactivity in the crystal.) Gentry, who has studied halos in some detail[10, 11, 12] reports:

> Further, by virtue of the very short half-life (of radio-activity associated with halos), the radioactivity and formation of the rocks must be almost instantaneous. Incredible? Perhaps. I have been wondering about this idea for some time, and have often asked myself: Is it conceivable that one of the oldest cosmological theories known to man is correct after all? Could the earth have been created by fiat? . . . The unusual halos, therefore, apparently do constitute evidence of primordial extinct short half-life radioactivity, and hence have a direct bearing not only on cosmologic theory but also on the presently accepted geologic time scales derived primarily from radioactive transformation rates. Geologically speaking, it is usually assumed that all the igneous rock of the earth's crust is of volcanic origin, but if the fiat creation hypothesis is correct, then the rock systems in which the variant short half-life halos are found would constitute the earth's primordial matter formed *in situ*.[13] (emphasis his)

Thus we see that data from the study of pleochroic halos strongly seems to suggest that the earth was formed almost instantaneously by Divine fiat.

---

[9] Patrick M. Hurley: *How Old Is the Earth?* (Doubleday & Company, Inc., Garden City, New York, 1959) p. 12.

[10] Robert V. Gentry: *Applied Physics Letters*, Vol. 8, 1966, p. 65.

[11] _____: *Earth, Plan, Sci. Lett.*, Vol. 1, 1966, p. 453.

[12] _____: *Bull. Amer. Phys. Soc.*, Vol. 12, 1967, p. 32.

[13] _____: Cosmology and Earth's Invisible Realm," *Medical Opinion and Review,* Vol. 3, No. 10, October 1967, p. 64-79.

It is also of interest in connection with the study of pleochroic halos in the same article that Gentry reports that there seems to be some indication that radioactive rates of decay may not always have been constant during geologic time. The implication of this for radioactive dating studies is obvious. Gentry writes:

> . . . my investigations of the uranium and thorium halos disclosed a startling circumstance: the radioactive decay rates had probably changed considerably during geologic time.[14]

Returning to the other part of our question, that of how long ago the Creation took place or how much time has elapsed since the beginning of geologic time, the inductive method will again be of help. The inductive method assists in making those assumptions most nearly in accord with known facts. Then with these assumptions deductive thinking will allow the data to be interpreted so that a measure of time in years since the beginning may be made. Again, since assumptions will always be involved, it is not possible to absolutely state that conclusions drawn are the only ones. We place our confidence in them because they seem to be the most probable ones.

Age of the Earth — Helium Dating

One method for making assumptions for estimating an upper limit to the number of years since the beginning of geologic time is based on the amount of accumulated decay products. All elements found in natural sources with atomic number greater than 83 (bismuth) are radioactive. The heavier elements decay and eventually become one of the stable isotopes of the element lead. Mass is lost in the form of alpha particles which ultimately become helium atoms. Helium gas then is a principle decay product of the heavier radioactive elements. This fact can be used to estimate an upper limit for the age of the earth.

As an example, the relative abundances of the elements thorium and helium would seem to indicate that an assumed figure of the order of 10^{10} years (ten billion) for the age of the earth is very much too great. If this figure were correct, about one half-life would have elapsed for thorium 232 decay. This means that the present amount of thorium on earth is one-half the original amount. In other words, the present amount of thorium is equal to the amount which has decayed. In decaying, however, thorium 232 eventually becomes a stable isotope, lead 208 while producing 6 helium atoms.

[14]*Ibid.*

Hence, since on this assumption the present amount of thorium is equal to the amount which has decayed, helium ought to be about six times as abundant as thorium, even assuming no other elements than thorium were radioactive (which is not the case) and assuming no helium was present to start with (which is very unlikely considering the high relative abundance of helium in the cosmos.) This is not the case as helium on the earth is quite rare. The proper amount of helium for ages assumed to be of the order of billions of years is simply not present either in the rocks or in the atmosphere assuming it to have escaped from the rocks somehow.

While discussing the helium clock for measuring the age of the earth, Faul states:

> There was a time, just before World War II, when the helium clock looked very promising. In time it became apparent, however, that many of the early indications were misleading and that it was difficult to find systems consistently closed to helium.[15]

In other words, the amount of helium that ought to have been present as a decay product in terms of non-creation old age earth assumptions simply was not there. The non-Creationists' (i.e., naturalists') explanation for failing to find the facts in agreement with old earth assumptions was to postulate that the helium had escaped somehow. Rather than take the facts at face value, an excuse was made as to why the "clock" was in error. Hurley also discusses this point. He writes:

> Another discovery was to be of much interest in the question of earth age. This was that helium, first found on the sun and then on earth, was a product of the breakdown of uranium and thorium. It was another of the tools that, early in this century, enabled scientists to make their initial attempts to measure earth age through the process of radioactivity. The great Lord Rutherford was the first to study the relation of helium to uranium in minerals, but the helium loss in the highly radioactive minerals he measured was so large his results indicated very low ages.[16]

Again, the data taken at face value give low ages, so it is proposed that the clock is reading incorrectly because the helium has escaped. The rate of helium escape has not necessarily been measured. It is merely presumed in order to explain why the data is not as expected. Investigations of the rate of loss of helium from

---

[15]Henry Faul, *op. cit.*, p. 20.
[16]Patrick M. Hurley, *op. cit.*, p. 87.

minerals cast considerable doubt on this type of explanation. Fanale and Schaeffer comment:

> Studies of the helium method have shown that low ages based on helium, obtained on common rock-forming minerals do not necessarily reflect diffusive loss of helium from the lattices of those minerals; under ideal conditions, some mineral lattices even appear to retain helium quantitatively for longer than 10^8 years.[17]

Cook has made some calculations on the upper limit for the age of the earth based on helium, and arrives at a figure of 12,000 years.[18] If 12,000 years is the *maximum* age of the earth and we use a value of 5,000 years for a *minimum* age, this means that the true age is somewhere between these two figures. It is obvious that by taking the facts as we find them, one can arrive at an upper limit for the age of the earth and geologic time which is considerably different from the 4-½ billion years of the non-Creation approach.

Data from most of the other common radioactive dating methods seem to be open to no more absolute interpretation than the helium clock method. Other methods are also entirely dependent on assumptions. Further postulates that material has either been added or lost are made whenever the facts do not agree with what old-age-earth thinking expects them to be. A few quotes should serve to illustrate the point. Faul comments concerning potassium-argon dating:

> It is difficult to be certain whether a significant amount of environmental argon was originally enclosed in any K-Ar system used for age determination because there is no basis for estimating the isotopic composition of original argon.[19]

Again, Faul writes:

> The amount of original argon can be deduced only by comparing the measured K-Ar "age" with other ages; hence, it may be difficult to decide whether some of the observed "original argon" may not actually be a recent loss of potassium.[20]

In discussing the geologic time scale, Faul writes:

> Any absolute geologic time scale must be built up by interpolating between suitable events that can be not only dated in absolute

[17]F. P. Fanale and O. A. Schaeffer, *Science*, Vol. 149, July 1965, p. 312.
[18]Melvin A. Cook: *"Prehistory and Earth Models"* (London, Max Parrish, 1966), p. 14.
[19]Henry Faul, *op. cit.*, p. 32.
[20]*Ibid.* p. 46.

terms but also accurately placed in the relative time of stratigraphy.
. . . Rocks that are suitable for age measurement and at the same
time reliably correlated with the stratigraphic sequence are very
rare.[21]

Faul continues:

Uraniferous shale is another unreliable system. In several parts of
the world are large shale deposits with fairly high uranium con-
tents. Their stratigraphic position is accurately known, but these
rocks are not closed systems. Uranium and lead both migrate in
them in geologic time, and detailed analyses have shown that useful ages cannot be obtained from them. Similar difficulties prevail
in attempts to date pitchblende veins. Here again much chemical
activity is known to take place and widely diverging "ages" can be
measured on samples from the same spot.[22]

It may well be true that geochemical alteration has happened in
certain situations which has the effect of making the time measured
by radioactive clock meaningless. One wonders, though, if it is
justifiable to invoke this mechanism whenever facts are not as
expected. Sometimes it almost seems that much of the emphasis
placed on the assertion that radio-dating verifies the long-age-
geological-time-scale may be only a smoke screen to prevent the
scientific layman from exercising his right to challenge the basic
assumptions of non-Creationist thinking.

The fact that these assumptions are open to challenge seems
to be emphasized even by the ones who hold to the old earth
ideas. Tilton and Steiger write:

. . . the age calculation also contains the assumption that the
isotopic composition of lead in the earth was initially the same
as that in the troilite phase of iron meteorites. This assumption
may be incorrect.[23]

Faul further emphasizes the vulnerability of age schemes to the
basic assumptions. He states

Much geologic insight into the origin and history of ores can be
gained from judicious interpretation of the isotopic composition of
lead, *but colossal misconceptions can arise from false assumptions*.[24] (emphasis mine)

---

[21]*Ibid.* p. 52-53.
[22]*Ibid.* p. 61.
[23]G. R. Tilton, and R. H. Steiger, *Science*, Vol. 150, 31 December 1965,
    p. 1807.
[24]Henry Faul, *op. cit.* p. 69.

I would like to suggest that perhaps one of these misconceptions is that the earth is billions of years old. Cook at least after examining several lines of evidence such as radioactive dating has been able to show that assumptions leading to a young earth are in accord with the facts. He suggests a maximum age of around 12,000 years and concludes:

> . . . a very interesting implication of this study is that not only are the sedimentary rocks relatively young, but also, therefore, are their occluded fossils. This implication, based on what the author considers to be hard facts, has an important bearing on the prehistory of life.[25]

It is obvious that the fossils in the rocks cannot be older than the rocks. If the earth has an age measured in thousands of years so do the fossils.

Conclusion

We have examined two questions in this chapter. First, the idea that the earth is very, very old is not in any way suggested by any studies in science. It arises as a result of rejecting Special Creation. Second, the facts of science must be interpreted. The acceptance or rejection of the Genesis account correlates closely with the assumptions used in interpreting the data.

The facts themselves do set some limits, though, on what assumptions are reasonable. These reasonable assumptions lead to the conclusion that Genesis is actual history and that the earth was created by fiat and not so very long ago. An age of six to seven thousand years is not unreasonable and allows one to accept at face value such data as the helium clocks.

To reject Special Creation, one has to step outside the area of human experience and in addition one must continue to make excuses whenever following data from the real world to its logical conclusion. One must relinquish, it would seem, the claim to truth and in effect embrace an error or a falsehood. The Scripture says:

> The fear of the Lord is the beginning of knowledge: but fools despise wisdom and instruction (Proverbs 1:7).

Again:

> The fool has said in his heart, "There is no God" (Psalm 53:1).

---

[25]Melvin A. Cook, *op. cit.* p. XIV.

The core of the issue then is not the age of the earth or fossils. Rather, it is the recognition and honor of God, the Creator. He has provided a record and revelation for man both from the realm of the created world and the written Word. Will one be foolish and reject this revelation or be wise and continue to be instructed?

A Scriptural Groundwork for
Historical Geology

Stuart E. Nevins

STUART E. NEVINS

From a very early age, Mr. Nevins has had a continued interest in geology. At the age of ten he appeared on San Francisco television several times because of his ability in science. His field work has been extensive, having observed geologic structures in every western state except Alaska and Hawaii. During 1966 he received a National Science Foundation stipend through the University of Colorado, and worked in the field of glacial geology.

He earned the Eagle Scout Award with Bronze Palm, and the God and Country Award, in Scouting. Later he received the Vigil Honor in the Order of the Arrow, and was elected as National Secretary of the Knights of Dunamis for a one-year term. He lectures on campuses and in churches on earth history and the Bible, and is a campus leader with the Navigators.

IV

A SCRIPTURAL GROUNDWORK FOR
HISTORICAL GEOLOGY

The earth has long captured a special fascination of human thought. For thousands of years men have marvelled at the mountains, the rivers, the plains and the oceans. Men have wondered about the weather, the soil, the strata and the fossils. Observations of the earth's features have led to a widened understanding of the many processes of nature. Men of later times have increasingly become more aware of their physical world. Recent generations have attempted to systematize the existing knowledge, to make new observations, to draw further interpretations, and to communicate these to other people. Within the past two hundred years the facts relating to the earth's crust have become so numerous that an organized field of knowledge has developed called *geology*.

Today the scope of geology is extremely widespread, encompassing many specialized subfields. Among the best known are mineralogy (the study of minerals), petrology (the study of the origin and characteristics of rocks), stratigraphy (the study of surface accumulated rocks), and structural geology (the study of folded and faulted rocks).

Geology includes subfields related also to other studies. Among these are geophysics (physics applied to the study of the earth's forces and phenomena), geochemistry (chemistry applied to the materials of the earth), geomorphology (the study of the configurations of the earth's surface features — relates also to geography), hydrology (the study of the circulation of the earth's water), and paleontology (the study of fossil organisms — relates also to biology).

For convenience, the whole field of geology has been broken down into two separate branches — *physical geology* which studies the earth's present character, and *historical geology* which deals with the earth's history. Physical geology directly studies processes which are presently observable, which can be directly seen in the "laboratory" of nature. Reproducibility of observation is a requirement of physical geology. Because it studies presently visible objects and events, physical geology can be called a *science*.

With historical geology, however, ancient events are studied which cannot be reproduced. Earth history is not presently seen. For these reasons the historical geologist relies on *indirect* evidence to understand past events. He can never directly see the operation of past processes, but only clues of their action preserved in the rocks. Often massive amounts of speculation must be considered by the historical geologist before an adequate theory can be proposed. His conclusions must necessarily incorporate assumptions which relate past events to those presently seen. The methods used do not rest on scientific principles. Historical geology *cannot be strictly called a science* because it does *not* deal with events which are presently visible and susceptible to experimental study.

The Bible and Geology

Many of the Biblical authors displayed a remarkable understanding of the physical structure of the earth. For example, Job said, "He [God] . . . hangeth the earth upon nothing" (Job 26:7). We know this to be correct, that the earth is unsupported in space. In Job 38:6 God questioned Job about the foundations of the earth, "Where upon are the foundations thereof fastened?" The Hebrew word "foundations" in the sixth verse is designated "sockets" and the word "fastened" is given literally in the margins of many Bibles as "made to sink." Did Job have some idea of how the continents are fastened? Within the past thirty-five years seismic evidence has been available to indicate a roughly horizontal discontinuity in the composition of the earth at a depth of several miles. Geologists believe that the continental portions of the crust are indeed fastened in depressed "sockets" which penetrate into the mantle lying below the discontinuity. Scholars prior to the sixteenth century believed the earth to be supported by various foundations (pillars, animals, etc.) but only recently have scientists agreed with Job who suggested that the earth unsupported in space yet as concerning continental shields, is fastened from within in sockets.

About 600 B.C. Jeremiah knew that the stars were innumerable. He said, "As the host of heaven cannot be numbered, neither the sand of the sea measured" (Jeremiah 33:22). The Greek astronomer Hipparchus in the second century B.C. concluded from his observations that there were less than 3,000 stars. Later the author of Hebrews reaffirmed the statement of Jeremiah, ". . . as the stars of the sky in multitude, and as the sand which is by the seashore innumerable" (Hebrews 11:12). In the second century A.D. Ptolemy, the great Egyptian scientist, counted 1,056 stars. He agreed with Hipparchus that there could be no more than 3,000 stars. The disagreement was resolved by the development of modern telescopes. Astronomers have seen billions of stars and are still discovering new galaxies containing billions of stars.

Isaiah apparently understood that the earth was spherical or rounded and that the atmosphere formed a "tent" or gauze "curtain" providing a protected environment for life (Isaiah 40:22). Solomon had an unbelievable knowledge of the wind systems and the water-vapor cycle of our planet (Ecclesiastes 1:6, 7). The distilling process forming rain was reported in Job 36:27, 28. Many Biblical authors displayed a remarkable understanding of the laws of thermodynamics which have been formally recognized within the last 150 years.

The Bible not only has statements of amazing scientific accuracy but also of crucial historical importance. The space and time transactions of God with man form the basic doctrines of the Bible. Unlike the Greek and Oriental authors who considered that history was cyclic and eternal, the Biblical authors report a unique sequence to historical events with a definite beginning and ending. Genesis relates not a timeless and mythical tale, but an account of a relatively recent and finished creation followed by a fall into sin and death. Later a universal flood engulfed the earth. Most of the Old Testament concerns God's dealings with the nation Israel. Eyewitnesses in the New Testament claim that God Himself took a body and lived on the earth for a short time. Atonement is offered through the crucifixion of Christ and salvation through His resurrection. A catastrophic eschatology is related in which the present heavens and earth will be replaced by new heavens and a new earth. The credibility of the entire Bible rests on the accuracy of its unique historical narrative.

However, historical geologists today feel that the history of the earth should be interpreted from evidence without particular regard for the historical statements of Scripture. Principles of investigation and interpretation, they suppose, should be derived solely from within the field of geology. The exclusively recognized fundamental assumption basic to popular historical geology is called the *Principle of Uniformity*. According to the Principle of Uniformity, *presently observed* geologic processes and scientific laws can explain *past* geologic events. The present, it is supposed, is the key to the past. "Fantastic" explanations such as creation or catastrophes are excluded from consideration in historical geology by the Principle of Uniformity. (Creation does not follow known scientific laws and catastrophes do not approximate present-day process rates.)

Not only does the Principle of Uniformity fail to incorporate Biblical history; it also does not follow scientific procedure. Sci-

ence requires that principles and laws be repeatedly tested. The
Principle of Uniformity defies direct testing because the natural
processes it identifies are not presently observable. The scientifically unsubstantiated basis of historical geology is emphasized
by the Harvard professor of geology William M. Davis:

> The very foundation of our science is only an *inference;* for the
> whole of it rests on the *unprovable assumption* that, all through
> the *inferred* lapse of time which the *inferred* performance of *in-
> ferred* geological processes involves, they have been going on in a
> manner consistent with the laws of nature as we know them now.
> *We seldom realize the magnitude of that assumption.* A phi-
> losopher of the would-be absolute school once said to me, in effect:
> "You geologists have an easy way of solving difficult questions:
> you account for the structures of the earth's crust by assuming that
> time and processes have been going on for millions and millions of
> years in the past as they go on today; but how do you know that
> time did not begin only a few hundred thousand years ago after
> the earth had been suddenly created in imitation of what it would
> have been if it had been slowly constructed in the manner that
> you assume?" The answer is as easy as the question: *We do not
> know; we merely make a pragmatic choice* between the concept
> of such an imitative creation which *seems* to us absurd, and the
> long and orderly evolution which *seems* to us reasonable.[1]

The basis, then, of today's historical geology does not rest in
science or scientific principles, nor in Biblical history, but in
naturalistic assumption.

Most educated people have some acquaintance with the apparent
problem areas between the Bible and science. Probably the best
known controversy concerns creation versus evolution. Today many
scientists feel that matter and energy have long existed in one form
or another. The present structure of the earth is thought to have
formed by a slow and continuous evolutionary process operating in
accordance with present natural causes over a period of several
billion years. The possibility of catastrophic events during this
evolutionary development is rejected. Characteristic of this limited
thinking is the reliance on the Principle of Uniformity as a basic
assumption.

Almost directly counter to the evolutionary cosmology is the
Biblical account which repeatedly states that God was responsible
for creating all things (Genesis 1:1; Psalm 146:6; Jeremiah 10:12;
Acts 4:24; etc.) Creation was also completed (Genesis 2:1-3;

---

[1]"The Value of Outrageous Geological Hypothesis," *Science*, Vol. 63,
1926, pp. 465, 466. Emphasis is ours.

Exodus 20:11; Hebrews 4:3, 10). If creation was completed and finished, then the means used to create are not presently operating in nature. Biblical statements and the assumption of uniformity can hardly be reconciled.

Not as well known, but still vitally important, is the problem of the Flood. The Biblical writers describe a universal catastrophe during which the waters covered "*all* the high hills, that were under the *whole* heaven" (Genesis 7:19). The Principle of Uniformity sternly rejects any catastrophic event like the Flood. Also, the miraculous resurrection of Christ cannot be considered seriously from the assumptions of historical geology because nothing similar is occurring today. The possibility of Christ's return is also held in disrepute by scientists who adhere strictly to the Principle of Uniformity.

While scientific statements of Scripture are remarkably accurate, there has been little agreement between the Bible's historical statements and historical geology. Any person informed on the present dichotomy between "science" and the Bible must know that historical geology consistently denies the historical statements of Scripture. Experimental science, however, has little quarrel with Biblical statements. (Only very minor points of disagreement remain where our understanding of either science or Scripture is inadequate.) In the final analysis, all areas of difficulty between "science" and the Bible appear to involve the historical statements of Scripture and the "science" founded upon the Principle of Uniformity. Even the problem of miracles, long thought to involve the physical sciences, relates to basic assumptions in historical geology.

What is this principle which remains separate from true science, yet so basic to historical geology? How was it developed and how is it used?

Historical Development

One of the greatest mind-shaking concepts ever to be introduced to the educated world was the Principle of Uniformity. Its establishment into the stream of scientific thought caused one of the greatest intellectual revolutions of all time. James Hutton (1726-1797), a Scottish doctor and agriculturalist, in 1788 formally presented the view that the entirety of geologic history was characterized by the uniform process rates and unchangeable laws which we are acquainted with today. According to Hutton, there was little need to consider catastrophes or divine intervention as important in geologic history. He wrote:

> Therefore, there is no occasion for having recourse to any unnatural supposition of evil, to any destructive accident in nature, or

to the agency of any preternatural cause, in explaining that which actually appears.[2]

George Cuvier (1769-1832), a French comparative anatomist, could not agree. His work with fossils and strata led him to believe that the history of life was interrupted at least five times by great watery catastrophes followed by periods of special creation. William Buckland (1784-1856), a theologian, holding what was the prevailing view during the eighteenth and early nineteenth centuries, thought that a special creation by God, and Noah's Flood recorded in Genesis, had distinct geologic significance. A bitter argument arose between these men and others later leading to the coining of the distinction "uniformitarians" and "catastrophists." The uniformitarians considered that process rates were unchanging and that there was no interruption of natural law by divine intervention. To the catastrophists past process rates differed significantly from present rates. Most of the catastrophists allowed supernaturalism but felt that natural laws had not changed since creation. The uniformitarians considered the earth to be extremely old while to the catastrophists the earth could have an age as young as 6000 years.

Defending the uniformitarian school of thought was Charles Lyell (1797-1875), a British lawyer, who wrote a series of volumes called *Principles of Geology*. Lyell's work made it clear that geology could develop an understanding of past events by observing present processes. His work gave exclusive credit to the uniformitarian view.

Other men worked with Lyell and his assumptions to develop the standard geologic column with major divisions organized upon paleontological evidence. Charles Darwin later made the Principle of Uniformity a basic assumption for interpreting the past evolutionary history of life. By 1865 the field of historical geology had been well oriented into its present evolutionary-uniformitarian framework. The uniformitarians using geologic evidence, logic and simplicity had succeeded, it appeared, in eliminating both supernaturalism and catastrophism from geology.

Thus the system introduced by Hutton, popularized by Lyell, and later adopted by Darwin, has remained largely unchanged for over one hundred years. The Principle of Uniformity has long been assumed to be the ultimate measure of newly developed geologic,

---

[2]"Theory of the Earth; or an Investigation of the Laws Observable in the Composition, Dissolution and Restoration of Land Upon the Globe," *Royal Soc. Edinburgh Trans.*, Vol. 1, 1788, p. 285.

biologic and astronomic theory. The history of life and the origin of the universe have long been presumed from uniformitarian and evolutionary assumptions. The influence of uniformitarianism has also been felt in the social sciences and humanities. Even man's concept of God is said to have evolved. Uniformitarianism has become an all-embracing principle!

It is noteworthy that a recent introductory biology text devotes a page to the description of the principle.

> There is an important principle fundamental for paleontology, geology, or any science that has historical aspects: the present is a key to the past. That principle was the subject of bitter controversy a century or two ago, when it was endowed with the formidable name of *the doctrine of uniformitarianism*. It is now accepted as true by virtually all scientists, and without it there could be no really scientific study of any kind of history. . . . The timelessness of the properties and processes of the universe was by no means obvious to earlier thinkers. Establishment of that principle was one of the major triumphs in the history of human thought.[3]

However, the widespread acceptance of the Principle of Uniformity has not been without its problems. Efforts to define and apply the principle have been quite perplexing. Hutton summed it up as "the present is the key to the past." This often repeated metaphor has led to much confusion. Is the Principle of Uniformity to be interpreted as applying to present and past process rates and material conditions, or present and past laws? Or is it just a "key" to the logic used by the geologist? Does the principle apply for all geologic time? With what success has the principle been used in solving geologic problems?

The vague and ambiguous character of the Principle of Uniformity has resulted from a lack of response to the above questions and the failure to distinguish the various types of uniformity. While the principle has been staunchly assumed by the uniformitarians for over one hundred years, a logical basis defending the principle has not been developed. The subject has been almost totally neglected by geologists. The history of science Professor Reijer Hooykaas, of Free University, Amsterdam, has said:

> The history of uniformitarianism has never been written; its philosophical examination has been restricted to a few articles: there

---

[3]G. G. Simpson and William S. Beck, *Life — An Introduction to Biology*, Harcourt, Brace & World, New York, 1965, p. 757. Emphasis is theirs.

exists no monograph on this fundamental principle of the "historical" natural sciences. It seems, therefore, useful to give a critical
analysis of its implications.[4]

Claude C. Albritton, Jr., geologist, from Southern Methodist University, has said:

> "The present is the key to the past," we say. The principle of
> uniformity, to which this adage refers, is held by many to be the
> foundation stone of geology. With regard to the validity of the
> principle, however, the range of opinion is amazing. . . . Geolo-
> gists and other scientists have such varied opinions on the matter
> that it would be impossible, without a vote, to say which view
> prevails. Surely the principle of uniformity needs the critical at-
> tention of geologists.[5]

Scientists have always attempted to generalize from their observations and to show the step-by-step methods used in reaching
conclusions. The need in geology to show the logical development
of ideas has always been critical, but not until recently has a con-
certed effort been made. Within the past ten years geologists,
historians of science and philosophers have done much to clarify
the Principle of Uniformity. One of the most significant steps taken
recently has been the recognition of the principle's two-fold character. Hooykaas has said:

> In many discussions about the principle of uniformity a certain
> vagueness arises because no distinction is made between two ele-
> ments contained therein, an ambiguity already present in Lyell's
> expositions.[6]

The distinction made by Hooykaas has been between "causes"
and "effects." The Principle of Uniformity seems to relate present
natural laws to past natural laws (present "causes" to past "causes")
and to relate present processes to past processes (present "effects" to past "effects"). The point has been further amplified
by Stephen Jay Gould, a Columbia University geologist, and
names have been given to both notions.

> Uniformitarianism is a dual concept. Substantive uniformitarianism
> (a testable theory of geologic change postulating uniformity of

---

[4]*The Principle of Uniformity in Geology, Biology and Theology,* second
impression, E. J. Brill, Leiden, Netherlands, 1963, p. XII.
[5]*The Fabric of Geology,* C. C. Albritton, Jr., Ed., Freeman, Cooper & Co.,
Stanford, California, 1963, p. 263.
[6]*Op. cit.,* p. 32.

rates or material conditions) is false and stifling to hypotheses formation. Methodological uniformitarianism (a procedural principle asserting spatial and temporal invariance of natural laws) belongs to the definition of science and is not unique to geology.[7]

Gould's division of the Principle of Uniformity into substantive uniformitarianism (uniformity of process rates or material conditions) and methodological uniformitarianism (invariance of natural law) has been of great value in resolving the problem.

Uniformity and Catastrophism

Hutton and Lyell both believed that process rates and material conditions were unchanging. Lyell supported substantive uniformitarianism when he wrote:

> If in any part of the globe the energy of a cause appears to have decreased, it is always probable that the diminution of intensity in its action is merely local, and that its force is unimpaired, when the whole globe is considered.[8]

The idea allowed the early uniformitarians to deny catastrophism, the belief in sudden upheavals. But as Gould has said, "substantive uniformitarianism . . . is false and stifling to hypotheses formation." An enormous body of evidence has accumulated since the founding of geology which has discredited the substantive uniformitarian view.

Over a hundred years of geologic research has correlated and superimposed rock strata producing the standard geologic column. Assembled upon uniformitarian assumptions to show the gradual evolution of life, it bears better testimony of catastrophism! Norman D. Newell, the very qualified paleontologist for the American Museum of Natural History, has compiled the stratigraphic distribution of some 2,250 animal families and has plotted their per cent extinction throughout the standard geologic column. The result of this study is the graph shown in Figure 7.

Rather than showing a uniform distribution of extinction and proliferation with time, the graph apparently shows that mass extinction and proliferation were confined to relatively brief episodes. As Newell comments:

---

[7]"Is Uniformitarianism Necessary?" *American Journal of Science,* Vol. 263, 1965, p. 223.

[8]*Principles of Geology,* first edition, John Murray, London, Vol. 1, 1830, pp. 164, 165.

One cannot doubt that there were critical times in the history of animals. Widespread extinctions and subsequent revolutionary changes in the course of animal life occurred roughly at the end of the Cambrian, Ordovician, Devonian, Permian, Triassic and Cretaceous periods. Hundreds of minor episodes of extinction occurred on a more limited scale at the level of species and genera throughout geologic time, but here we shall restrict our attention to a few of the more outstanding mass extinctions.[9]

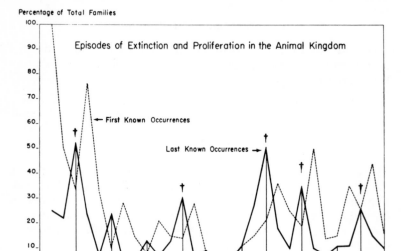

Percentage of Total Families

Episodes of Extinction and Proliferation in the Animal Kingdom

← First Known Occurrences

Last Known Occurrences →

CAM. | ORD. | SIL. | DEV. | MISS. | PENN. | PERM. | TRIAS. | JURA. | CRET. | CEN.

FIGURE 7. Episodes of extinction and proliforation of animal families through geologic time. Rather than showing a uniform rate of first and last appearance, the evidence of the fossil record indicates that extinction and proliferation were confined to relatively brief episodes. The major extinctions occurred near the end of the following periods: Cambrian (52 per cent extinction), Devonian (30 per cent extinction), Permian (50 per cent extinction), Triassic (35 per cent extinction), Cretaceous (26 per cent extinction). However, a new principle developed later in the text indicates that the evidence of the fossil record may be better understood as the result of a *single* catastrophe.

(After Newell, "Revolutions in the History of Life," G.S.A. Special Paper No. 89, 1967, p. 79.)

---

[9]"Crises in the History of Life," *Scientific American*, vol. 208, No. 2, 1963, p. 79.

Probably the most remarkable of the extinctions occurred at the end of the Permian period. Newell says:

> At or near the close of the Permian period nearly half of the known families of animals throughout the world disappeared . . . 75 per cent of amphibian families and more than 80 per cent of the reptile families had also disappeared.[10]

Newell further states:

> It is striking that times of widespread extinction generally affected many quite unrelated groups in separate habitats. The parallelism of extinction between some of the aquatic and terrestrial groups is particularly remarkable.[11]

Thus, the fossil record with its evidence of sudden disappearance of one assemblage of animal life followed by the abrupt superposition of different animal forms presents one of the greatest problems for substantive uniformitarianism.

Darwin, who considered that the evolution of life occurred by a slow and continuous process, attributed the apparent discontinuity of the record to incompleteness.

> Geology assuredly does not reveal any such finely-graduate organic chain; and this, perhaps, is the most obvious and serious objection which can be urged against the theory (Darwin's theory of organic evolution). The explanation lies, as I believe, in the extreme imperfection of the geological record.[12]

Darwin's concept of the "extreme imperfection of the geological record" is valid only when considering a local succession of strata. Correlation and superposition of strata from all over the world has produced the standard geologic column which today is thought to be fairly complete. For example, geologists have failed to find evidence of a missing stratigraphic interval during which the dinosaurs slowly became extinct. The Mesozoic-Cenozoic boundary where the dinosaurs disappear forms an abrupt separation of fauna. J. A. Jeletzky of the Geologic Survey of Canada considers that boundary as "natural" — not reflecting any great break in time.

> Speaking in geochronological terms, it follows from the above discussion that the Mesozoic-Cenozoic (or Cretaceous-Tertiary) boundary, as defined above, is a "natural" boundary based on a

---

[10]*Ibid.*
[11]*Ibid.*
[12]*Origin of Species*, D. Appleton & Co., New York, Vol. 2, 1890, p. 49.

unique and easily recognizable, major biochronological event apparently reflecting some kind of radical, world-wide change in the physical regime of our planet. Such an event can be quite properly referred to as a "catastrophe" or "revolution."[13]

Observations from every continent are confirming the adequacy of the fossil record with many of its major "gaps" or boundaries reflecting rapid changes of environments rather than incomplete evidence of slow and uniform change.

Independent investigation on geologic problems has discredited the idea that today's rates and material conditions approximate those of the past. Geologic evidence has been available that suggests material conditions were much different from those observed today. Our presently high standing continents with lofty mountain chains can hardly be considered representative of past relief. Evidence of continental glaciation shows that a colder climate existed at one time. There is abundant geologic evidence of former catastrophic events. Rock formations show current structures which indicate that transcontinental flood conditions once prevailed. Critics of substantive uniformitarianism have found fossil graveyards, trees buried by massive lava flows, frozen mammoths in Arctic regions, and many other exceptions to a strict adherence to the substantive uniformitarian view. The great mass of evidence indicating catastrophe has been largely ignored by geologists.

Actually, the assumption that process rates must be uniform is without scientific backing. There is no scientific law which requires a natural event always to proceed at constant rate. A scientific law only describes an event under a fixed set of conditions and as conditions vary so does the rate. Conditions, not scientific law, determine the rate of a process. In laboratory experiments repeated accuracy is achieved by careful design which fixes, eliminates, or sufficiently reduces as many conditions as possible. But when one considers a process which is massive enough to be of geologic importance, the number of material conditions (a small change of any one factor could drastically alter the rate) is multitudinous. Factors may exist which scientists have not yet discovered. To insist that present rates or material conditions are average for all geologic time rests entirely upon uniformitarian assumption.

---

[13]"The Allegedly Danian Dinosaur-bearing Rocks of the Globe and the Problem of the Mesozoic-Cenozoic Boundary," *Journal of Paleontology*, vol. 36, 1962, p. 1010.

Another problem encountered is that substantive uniformitarianism has been at least partially inadequate as a basis for evolutionary theory. Lyell maintained that material conditions were essentially unchanging. Whereas Lyell denied any development, Darwin's evolutionary theory necessitated a developmental change in environments through time.

> All that can be said here is that if Darwin was deeply indebted to Charles Lyell for the method of accounting for large changes by summing up small changes over immense periods of time, nevertheless he did not accept the general Uniformitarian account of the history of nature. Evolution by means of natural selection involves the acceptance of the idea that some sort of cumulative development is demonstrated by geological and biological evidence — and it is just this idea that Uniformitarianism consistently denied.[14]

Because the uniformitarianism of Lyell was at least in part unacceptable to the early evolutionists, many philosophers of science consider that it was replaced by evolutionism. Indeed, evolutionary concepts, which contain a few of the acceptable assumptions of Lyell, appear to form the basis of today's historical geology. Albritton says:

> Most modern historians of science seem to agree that Lyell's famous principle was an a-historic device, which was discarded after evolutionism became popular in the nineteenth century. Most modern philosophers of science seem to feel either that the principle is too vague to be useful, or that it is an unwarranted and unnecessary assumption.[15]

Lyell has done more than any other man in bringing the historical sciences to their uniformitarian viewpoint. His fidelity to the constancy of rates and conditions has been unfavorably reviewed by recent authorites. Gould has said:

> Substantive uniformitarianism as a descriptive theory has not withstood the test of new data and can no longer be maintained in any strict manner.[16]

Nelson Goodman, an educator from Harvard, has affirmed:

> If the Principle of Uniformity is to be taken seriously, it cannot

---

[14]W. F. Cannon, "Uniformitarian — Catastrophist Debate," *Isis*, Vol. 51, 1960, p. 55.
[15]*Op. cit.*
[16]*Op. cit.*, p. 226.

be identified with any such blatant lie as that Nature remains always the same or moves only with dignity.[17]

A Princeton historian of science has said:

> Geologically, of course, Lyell's critics were right. No one now holds such extreme views upon the uniform course of nature.[18]

In the final analysis, the substantive uniformitarianism of Hutton and Lyell was an *a priori assumption* formed not upon evidence but upon a preconceived opinion of how nature must ideally operate if we are to study it by inductive means. Lyell's attempt to make historical investigation strictly equatable to scientific methods of testing compelled him to exclude catastrophic events. Yet subsequent research has confirmed that former rates and conditions have varied sizably from those we observe today. Even to evolutionists some portions of Lyell's substantive uniformitarianism are unacceptable.

Uniformity and Thermodynamics

Gould has divided the Principle of Uniformity into two separate concepts — substantive uniformitarianism (uniformity of process rates or material conditions) and methodological uniformitarianism (invariance of natural laws). Substantive uniformitarianism was originally proposed to discredit the idea of violent upheavals which had been very common prior to the middle nineteenth century. Yet, we have seen that geologists, philosophers and historians today are returning to the original notion. The present concern among evolutionists and uniformitarians is to reintroduce some forms of catastrophism while excluding the Biblicalism and supernaturalism widely held in the early nineteenth century. To do this the second concept embodied in the Principle of Uniformity, methodological uniformitarianism, has had to be restated recently. Gould's definition was:

> Methodological uniformitarianism (a procedural principle asserting spatial and temporal invariance of natural laws) belongs to the definition of science and is not unique to geology. Methodological uniformitarianism enabled Lyell to exclude the miraculous from

[17]"Uniformity and Simplicity," *Uniformity and Simplicity*, C. C. Albritton, Jr., Ed., Geological Society of America Special Paper #89, 1967, p. 93.

[18]Charles C. Gillispie, *Genesis and Geology*, Harper & Row, New York, 1959, p. 134.

geologic consideration; its innovation today is anachronistic since the question of divine intervention is no longer an issue in science.[19]

A Stanford geologist considered methodological uniformitarianism essential for interpreting geologic history. He regarded two assumptions as basic:

1. We assume that natural laws are invariant with time.
2. We exclude hypotheses of the violation of natural laws by Divine Providence, or other forms of supernaturalism.[20]

George Gaylord Simpson, the Harvard paleontologist, said:

The doctrine of geological uniformitarianism, finally established early in the 19th century, widened the recognized reign of natural law. The earth has changed throughout its history under the action of material forces, only, and of the *same* forces as those now visible to us and still acting on it.[21]

Hutton and Lyell also believed in the invariance of natural laws and denied supernaturalism. Lyell often made statements concerning the unchangeability of the laws of nature.

Our estimate, indeed of the value of all geological evidence, and the interest derived from the investigation of the earth's history, must depend entirely on the degree of confidence which we feel in regard to the permanency of the laws of nature. Their immutable constancy alone can enable us to reason from analogy, by the strict rules of induction, respecting the events of former ages, or, by a comparison of the state of things at two distinct geological epochs, to arrive at the knowledge of general principles in the economy of our terrestrial system.[22]

A statement of the uniformity of physical and chemical laws is indeed necessary for scientific investigation. Science depends upon the reproducibility of observation. Scientists, however, cannot safely extrapolate from present knowledge and require that natural laws have *always* operated as they do today. The denial of supernaturalism as an assumption is also without basis. In fact, some

---

[19]*Op. cit.*
[20]M. King Hubbert, "Critique of the Principle of Uniformity," *Uniformity and Simplicity*, G.S.A. Special paper #89, 1967, p. 30.
[21]"The World into Which Darwin Led Us," *Science*, Vol. 131, 1960, p. 967. Emphasis is his.
[22]*Op. cit.*, p. 165.

startling self-contradictions with the laws of science arise from assuming strict methodological uniformitarianism.

Two of the most basic and best proved laws of science are those of energy conservation and entropy. These two laws are more commonly referred to as the first and second laws of thermodynamics. The first law of thermodynamics (energy conservation) states that although energy can be changed from one form to another, the total quantity of energy is conserved (energy is presently neither being created nor destroyed). The second law of thermodynamics (entropy) affirms that any system left alone will become more random and disorganized. When a physicist, chemist, biologist or geologist studies any present process where energy is changing form, he feels certain that the quantity of energy before and after the event occurs is conserved, and that the quality of the energy after completion of the event is more random, diversified, and less able to do work. These two laws apply in present systems ranging from sub-nuclear to astronomic dimensions. Both laws have been confirmed without exception in thousands of experiments. The importance of thermodynamics as it relates to geologic and biologic problems is stated by a Princeton biologist:

> Chemical reaction is always associated with thermodynamic changes which determine the direction the reaction takes and how nearly it goes to completion. This is true whether the reaction goes on in a test tube, a geological formation, or in a living system; and must have been true in the infancy of our earth as well as today.[23]

If we could summarize the present character of the universe it would be in quantity *conservative* and in quality *decaying*.

The most basic contradiction within methodological uniformitarianism concerns the second law of thermodynamics. If the second law which describes the decay of present systems has always operated as today, the present universe would be completely dissipated of all energy sources and would lack density. Yet the things we observe today are still highly energized and ordered. *Therefore, we know that the second law of thermodynamics has not always operated.* The methodological uniformitarian who maintains the unchangeability of natural laws stands contradicted by one of the best proved laws of science!

Another difficulty attached to methodological uniformitarianism concerns origins. The accepted evolutionary theories explain the origin and integration of the present cosmos by causes in effect

---

[23]Harold F. Blum, *Time's Arrow and Evolution*, Princeton Univ. Press, Princeton, New Jersey, 1951, p. 14.

today. Indeed, this thinking forms the basis of the whole evolutionary system. Yet it is wishful thinking if the methodological uniformitarian believes that the origin and integration of the present cosmos can be explained by the present laws of conservation and decay. The fallacy is emphasized by Henry M. Morris, hydraulic engineer, of Virginia Polytechnic Institute:

> Consequently, it is fundamentally impossible for science to learn anything about origins. Science deals with present processes, and present processes are conservative, not creative. Thus, historical geology, professing to discover the history of the origin and evolution of the earth and its inhabitants through a scientific study and extrapolation of present processes, is a self-contradiction.[24]

In fact, the great difficulty of the evolutionary-uniformitarian system resulted from its acceptance before the significance of thermodynamics was recognized. Both Hutton and Lyell thought that the operation of present processes extended into a past of practically infinite geologic time. Hutton said:

> The result, therefore, of our present enquiry is that we find no vestige of a beginning — no prospect of an end.[25]

The idea that the earth was essentially a perpetual motion machine was challenged by Lord Kelvin (1824-1907) who helped formulate the second law of thermodynamics. Kelvin pointed out that the second law showed that the earth dissipated energy and, therefore, could not be eternally old.

When methodological uniformitarianism is strictly applied to all earth history, the result is self-contradiction. Thermodynamics has presented an understanding of nature different than that of the early uniformitarians. Yet a problem has not been resolved: how was the present cosmos formed if not according to present laws? The answer is found in considering that the creation of the universe preceded the establishment of the two laws of thermodynamics. The subject, however, is not a question for scientific consideration. Only the Creator can provide us with some understanding of how He made this world.

Uniformity and the Supernatural

When modern science as we know it today began to develop in the seventeenth century, men of science became aware that natural phenomena obeyed cause and effect relationships. Newton and

---

[24]"Science Versus Scientism in Historical Geology," *A Symposium on Creation*, Baker Book House, Grand Rapids, Michigan, 1968, p. 25.
[25]*Op. cit.*, p. 304.

others correctly thought that processes could be described by laws and considered the order and symmetry of nature at the same time rejecting older ideas postulating a lawless universe. While super-naturalism was not denied, it was recognized that it lay outside the realm of scientific investigation. The historicity of miracles was not questioned, but it appeared that the period of their occurrence was over. God was not needed in sustaining the *present* system for it operated according to natural laws which He had established. A mechanistic and deterministic view of nature began to develop with God's present role in *preserving* the universe under serious question.

Hutton lived in this climate of thought. To him the earth was a giant machine composed of three separate systems: lithosphere, hydrosphere, atmosphere. *All* geologic history he proposed could be explained by the interaction of the three systems. The operation of the earth's processes occurred through essentially unlimited time. The belief allowed Hutton to deny supernatural intervention in earth history. Not only did Hutton's view question God's *present* role in *preservation* of the universe, but also His *past* activity in *creation*. Indeed, Hutton believed that nature operated autonomously from a supernatural being.

While Buckland and others believed that God could have operated in earth history by providential intervention, Hutton and Lyell considered the unchangeability of natural law as basic in developing the infant study of geology.

> If Buckland feared that without cataclysms there was no God, Lyell was as fundamentally apprehensive lest, without uniformity, there be no science. He could feel no reverence for a lawgiver who kept amending the constitution of nature.[26]

Apparently Lyell's main reason for denying supernaturalism was to establish an inductive basis for historical geology.

Thus, through the efforts of Hutton, Lyell and other men an attitude was instilled into science which considered nature to be a closed system, operating as a machine governed by strict cause and effect relationships. The "immutable" laws proposed by the methodological uniformitarians seemed to rule the natural world.

> In science the significant change came about therefore as a result of a shift in emphasis from the uniformity of natural causes to the uniformity of natural causes in a closed system.[27]

---

[26]*Op. cit.*, p. 121.

[27]Francis A. Schaeffer, *Escape from Reason*, Inter-Varsity Press, Chicago, 1968, p. 37.

Methodological uniformitarianism, which arose from seventeenth and eighteenth century concepts of the uniformity of natural laws, made nature a self-sustaining machine always independent of supernatural influence.

> The uniformitarian school, in other words, is essentially a revolt against the Christian conception of time as limited and containing historic direction, with supernatural intervention constantly imminent. Rather this philosophy involves the idea of the Newtonian machine, self-sustaining and forever operating on the same principles.[28]

One difficulty encountered by the denial of supernaturalism concerns the confusion of natural law with scientific law. The exact procedure by which nature operates can be called natural law. The designation affirms our belief that nature is orderly, not chaotic. Scientific law is a generalization from many observations describing how nature operates. In every case scientific law is only a good approximation of natural law. While scientists have an equation which describes the motion of falling objects, they have no certainty that their equation is the only one which adequately describes the motion. In fact, there are a tremendous number of alternative equations (many extremely complex, having yet to be disproved) which describe the same motion.

Often scientific laws have to be revised to agree with new observations. The contradictory event does not demonstrate a miraculous occurrence but an inadequately formulated scientific law. By no means can the methodological uniformitarian draw conclusions on what can or what cannot be observed in nature. Our belief in the basic orderliness of nature is justified only as long as scientists succeed in writing laws descriptive of its behavior. Under no circumstances can scientists demand that a particular scientific law regulates natural events. The laws of science are *de*scriptive, not *pre*scriptive. They are statements of probability rather than statements of certainty. Scientists are unacquainted with what actually causes or controls natural phenomena. Thus, the possibility of God working, even by methods described by scientific laws, cannot be excluded from consideration.

Methodological uniformitarianism has been used to deny super-

---

[28]Loren Eiseley, *Darwin's Century,* Doubleday & Co., Garden City, New York, 1958, p. 114. Newton believed the *present* universe to be "self-sustaining," but Eiseley improperly adds: "forever operating on the same principles." Newton, like several of his associates, accepted the historicity of the Creation, the Flood and miracles.

naturalism in nature. The attack has been waged against God's role in both *preserving* and *creating* the cosmos. The first assertion is that God is no longer needed to sustain the *present* natural system because it is controlled by invariant laws. This concept, however, fails to recognize the descriptive (not controlling) character of scientific laws. Actually, scientists today are ignorant of what controls nature. The second assertion is that God is no longer needed during any *past* period of creation because the universe has *always* been controlled by invariant laws. This assumption fails to take into account the laws of thermodynamics. The second law of thermodynamics has not always operated. The first law (energy conservation) impresses the fallacy of attempting to explain creation in terms of present processes.

Thus, methodological uniformitarianism is an overly strict assumption. The uniformity of natural laws is necessary for scientific investigation but is false when strictly formulated as specifying the *invariance* of natural laws. The denial of supernaturalism is unwarranted.

Uniformity and Simplicity

Investigating observable facts and formulating laws which can be repeatedly demonstrated, science concerns itself only with a study of present natural properties and processes. Only events which can be seen or measured in the laboratory or in nature are susceptible to *scientific* investigation. Often great expense is incurred by the *scientific* fields of physics, chemistry, biology, astronomy, and *physical* geology for instruments used to extend our senses. But when we consider historical geology which deals with past processes, it becomes abundantly clear that this is not strictly science. Historical geology concerns itself with events which are *non-observable* and *non-repeatable*. Any investigation of past events must necessarily incorporate a set of assumptions relating present to past which can hardly be proved scientifically. The assumptions used by historical geologists during the last one hundred years have been recognized to be contained in the Principle of Uniformity.

Recently it has been noted that the Principle of Uniformity contains two concepts. Substantive uniformitarianism, the assumption that process rates and material conditions are unchanging, has been criticized. Its applicability to historical geology has been questioned.

Methodological uniformitarianism which assumes that laws are invariant through time has generally been well accepted among geologists. However, it has been recognized that this assumption, too, is not based upon observation. The idea that laws are invariant also has been criticized. Goodman says:

> A danger here lies in a fanciful notion of these laws as portent agencies exerting actual control over the course of events. Whatever made the world and whatever makes it go, the scientist writes its laws. And whether or not nature behaves according to law depends entirely upon whether we succeed in writing laws that describe its behavior. Once this is understood, the formula that laws now holding have held in the past and will hold in the future becomes either false or empty. Surely not *all* laws for any given period hold for other periods; we can always write special laws for a given stretch of time.[29]

Goodman concludes:

> Thus the Principle of Uniformity, construed as denying change or abrupt change in the course of the laws of nature can be rejected as false or futile.[30]

Lyell's book, *Principles of Geology*, is superficially an unbiased inquiry into how the present can be used to interpret the past. Upon closer examination, however, his assumptions are not verified by observation, but are staunchly defended in order to discredit the catastrophists. Two assumptions included in the Principle of Uniformity have been discussed and several implications of each explored. The many contradictions encountered make the Principle of Uniformity unacceptable to the historical geologist. The principle which has long been considered the basis for historical geology has been shown to be inadequate.

Therefore, a concept is being developed which is beginning to replace the Principle of Uniformity. It is called the *principle of simplicity*. Albritton says:

> The trend of opinion seems to be in the direction of identifying methodologic uniformity as a geological formulation of the logical principle of simplicity.[31]

Goodman says:

> Perhaps the first step toward clarifying the Principle of Uniformity of nature is to transform it into a principle of the simplicity of theory.[32]

---

[29]*Op. cit.*, p. 94. Emphasis is his.
[30]*Ibid.*
[31]"Uniformity, the Ambiguous Principle," *Uniformity and Simplicity*, G.S.A. Special Paper #89, 1967, p. 2.
[32]*Op. cit.*, p. 95.

When a natural event can be described in several different ways, the principle of simplicity merely states that the scientist should first consider the simplest description which agrees with the available evidence. The principle warns against needlessly multiplying explanations when a simple one is satisfactory. The principle directs all scientific endeavor but is not confined to science. We unconsciously use the principle of simplicity in our daily lives. While there are innumerable different routes to a particular destination, we choose the one which is shortest and least difficult. In the same way scientists take the shortest route in hope for truth.

The distinction between the Principle of Uniformity and the principle of simplicity should be noted. The Principle of Uniformity has been used to restrict natural occurrences. Lyell excluded catastrophism and supernaturalism in his assumptions. However, the principle of simplicity in no way limits nature, but only limits the scientist in his method of study. The principle of simplicity welcomes catastrophic interpretations of earth history as long as simplicity can be strictly maintained. Supernaturalism is not denied by the principle of simplicity.

Impressive evidence relating to the catastrophic extinction of life throughout the geologic column was presented in Figure 7, page 86. *Apparently* five major episodes of "mass extinction" occurred along with hundreds of minor episodes. Both marine and terrestrial animals seemed to have died out simultaneously. Geologists have offered many explanations for these extinctions: sudden changes in climate, bursts in cosmic radiation, changes in the salinity of the oceans, etc. Of course, each hypothesis has been very difficult to test from the fossil record. The amount of speculation continues to grow, but the proposals are either unsatisfactory or untestable. The search has been for a cause or causes which are both repetitive and world encompassing in their effect.

Another interpretation of the graph in Figure 7 (p. 86) is founded more directly upon the principle of simplicity. Rather than proposing hundreds of mass extinctions, each having different causes and effects, the principle of simplicity would suggest that we consider the evidence the result of a *single* catastrophe. The type of catastrophe is indicated by the abundance of fossils in water-deposited sedimentary rocks. Flood conditions are necessary. Abundant fossils form today under conditions of rapid burial. Flooding is the only known means of rapid deposition with widespread lateral extent. The simplest explanation, then, based on evidence from the fossil record is a single universal flood catastrophe.

While Norman D. Newell, who assembled the graph, may not

favor a single global catastrophe, he has expressed the need for
the use of the principle of simplicity in interpreting the extinctions.

> In the present state of knowledge, it seems to me to be more
> fruitful to seek a general explanation adequate to embrace many
> examples of mass extinction rather than to attempt a unique ex-
> planation for each episode. This is in better accordance with the
> known facts and satisfies the principle of simplicity of hypothesis.[33]

Thus, the principle of simplicity and consideration of the evidence of the fossil record logically establishes a catastrophe similar
to Noah's Flood recorded in Genesis. This hypothesis, however,
must be carefully tested only from evidence contained in the
rocks. By no means should the old argument of Lyell (substantive uniformitarianism) be used to deny the reality of the Flood.
In fact, this flood theory should retain top priority in the investigations of historical geologists since it is a simple theory which
adequately explains the fossil record.

The Scriptural Groundwork

Perhaps the greatest reason for denying the uniformitarian
system comes from an understanding of its appeal and promotion.
Man in his disobedience has rejected the knowledge of God and
has attempted to flee from His presence. Modern man, especially,
possesses an intellectual aversion to the supernatural. The Principle of Uniformity with its rejection of creationism and catastrophism has been widely heralded by skeptics and rationalists as the
foundation for historical geology. The principle seemingly frees
man from responsibility to his Maker and from the concern for any
future judgment or catastrophe. The point is illustrated by the
Apostle Peter's prophetic warning in II Peter 3:3-6:

> Knowing this first, that there shall come in the last days scoffers,
> walking after their own lusts, and saying, Where is the promise of
> his coming? for since the fathers fell asleep, all things continue as
> they were from the beginning of the creation. For this they will-
> ingly are ignorant of, that by the word of God the heavens were
> of old, and the earth standing out of water and in the water:
> Whereby the world that then was, being overflowed with water,
> perished.

Notice that these scoffers of the faith mentioned by Peter will
deny the possibility of a future judgment or catastrophe. They

---

[33]"Revolutions in the History of Life," *Uniformity and Simplicity*, G.S.A.
Special Paper #89, 1967, p. 82.

will say, "Where is the promise of his coming?" The reasoning used in doubting Christ's return will be based on the proposition that "all things *continue* as they were from the *beginning* of the creation." The assertion that everything keeps going as "from the beginning of the creation" maintains that present processes and laws have *always* operated. "Beginning of the creation" necessitates that even creation was accomplished by presently observable causes. God is, therefore, not needed in creation. The idea that present processes have always operated rejects the possibility that there was a flood catastrophe. Thus Peter, under God's inspiration, disapproved of the modern uniformitarian thinking in both its denial of creationism and catastrophism, and its adherence to present events to explain earth history.

One of the most important reasons for accepting the Biblical statements of earth history is the difficulty encountered without such a basis. Man's unaided intellectual endeavors cannot obtain all the answers. Scientific investigation fails to completely understand the preserved evidence in the rocks of the past events. Creation will always remain impervious to *scientific* investigation.

The historical geologist has long felt the need for a foundational truth upon which to base his study. In fact, most of the controversy in historical geology has related to defending basic principles. Efforts to establish historical geology on inductive principles which relate the present to the past have failed to account for the evidence of creation and catastrophe. Many of the concepts proposed by Hutton and Lyell have been shown to be full of gaps and inconsistencies. Therefore, if man is going to *know* the important events of the earth's creation and subsequent history, speculative assumptions cannot be used. Only an authoritative and historical record of events can furnish such a knowledge.

As we have analyzed the difficulties between some Biblical statements and historical geology, many of the areas of seeming conflict have been resolved. The Bible has demonstrated its trustworthiness as a basis for historical geology. The scriptural assertion of creation is now known to be consistent with the laws of thermodynamics. The claim that there was a flood catastrophe agrees with geologic evidence. With regard to the principle of simplicity the Biblical account offers the simplest proposal — a *single* creation and a *single* catastrophe.

Two concepts contained in the Principle of Uniformity have been examined. Substantive uniformitarianism, which has been used to reject catastrophic events like the Flood, has failed to stand up under new evidence. The fossil record, the laws of science and even modern evolutionary theory lend little support to the constancy of rates and conditions.

Methodological uniformitarianism, which has been used to deny God's role in both creating and preserving the universe, has been too strictly formulated. Contradictions are encountered with the laws of science by maintaining that natural causes have *always* operated. The denial of supernaturalism also fails to recognize the descriptive rather than controlling character of the laws of science.

The Principle of Uniformity, which has long been considered to be the foundation of historical geology, is inadequate. No longer can the historical geologist demand that nature must operate in a certain dignified manner. The demands are made upon the geologist as he seeks to study earth history.

There exists a critical need in historical geology today to re-examine principles and interpretations derived from uniformitarian assumptions. Especially do evolutionary theories and methods of age determination require special consideration in the light of new concepts. The basis and development of ideas must be shown. To this end the historical geologist should use the principle of simplicity and Biblical history to direct his investigation.

Genesis Time: A Spiritual Consideration

R. Clyde McCone

R. CLYDE McCONE

Dr. McCone is Associate Professor of Anthropology at California State College. Prior to accepting this position, he taught at Michigan State University, and South Dakota State College, and served as pulpit supply or pastor of a number of churches of different denominations in South Dakota and Montana.

Dr. McCone holds a B.A. in Religion from Wessington Springs College, a M.S. in Sociology from South Dakota State College, and a Ph.D. in Anthropology and Sociology from Michigan State University.

Dr. McCone was a participant in *Symposium on Creation* (I) with contributions entitled "Origins of Civilization," and "Evolutionary Time: A Moral Issue."

V

GENESIS TIME: A SPIRITUAL CONSIDERATION

The first few chapters of Genesis presents the reader with a rather extreme contrast. The creation of the incomprehensible vastness of the heavens and the earth is given in terms of days — just six days. The ages of the first man and his descendants are given in terms of centuries — almost a millennium. Within the culture of Western man these apparent temporal extremes have been called upon to answer two different questions. The first, "How long did it take God to create the heavens and the earth?" The second, "How long ago was it that He finished that creation?" There are other questions raised by the book of Genesis that have received less attention. This chapter is limited to these more neglected concerns. The first of these asks, "Did God create the universe in time, or is time an aspect of the universe which He created?"

Time and the Six Days of Creation

We understand first that these six days are days of creation and not re-creation. The second verse tells us that, "The earth was without form and void, and darkness was upon the face of the deep." Some understand by this verse that the original heavens and earth of Genesis 1:1 were destroyed. The six days would then be days of reconstruction. There are several reasons for believing that these six days are the six days of the original creation.

In the law, Moses refers to God as making the heavens and the earth in six days. At the close of the six days it is stated, "Thus the heavens and earth were finished and all the host of them." There is no reason to believe that the heavens and earth spoken of at the end of the six days of creation is a different heavens and earth than that mentioned in the first verse. Genesis 1:2 takes man back to the beginning and hence back to the Creator. Scriptures do this in the only manner that is possible for temporal man to grasp the "beginning." Without form is the absence of the structure of matter. Darkness is the absence of light — both physical and spiritual. Void is the absence of existence or being. God is saying in a way that the most simple can understand, "Before what is, was." What follows then is the revelation of God in six creative acts. Genesis 1:1 is a statement that in the beginning God created the heavens and the earth. The six days which follow are a revelation of the Creator and creation.

Secondly, we understand that since these are days of creation, they cannot be days of time. Day, as a unit of time measurement is a conception of man based on his observation of the regularity of the relative movements of the earth to other bodies in the universe, especially the sun. Since Genesis gives to us the origin of both man and the universe which he observes, creation can hardly be "measured" in days of time. In fact, time as modern man understands it, is an integral part with space and matter of the created universe. To read time into the account of creation, Genesis 1:1 would have to read, "In the beginning God created light and one day later he created the firmament, etc." Instead, we are told that, "In the beginning" the total universe is brought into being.

Also, if time is read into the creative account, there would be several problems regarding the order of the heavens and the earth. The earth would exist prior to the solar system of which it is a dependent part. There would be the growth of plant life without the light of the sun. Some have suggested the creation of light on the first day to be some kind of cosmic light and therefore plant life could live before the creation of the sun which is the important light-giving body for the earth. This conclusion comes from viewing creation as solely material.

Space, time and matter are the dimensions of a material universe. But man for whom this environment was created was more than material being. Into the molded dust of the ground God breathed His spirit. Therefore man's environment had to be both matter and spirit. The creation of light and its separation from darkness on the first day suggests the spiritual character of the universe. In I Timothy 6:16, Paul speaks of God as "dwelling in light that no man can approach unto." The realm of light in which man was intended to dwell was created. The line which the Creator has drawn between light and darkness is universal and unchanging. It also describes the moral environment in which man chooses, lives, moves, and has his being.

One further consideration about the days of creation is the Creator's day of rest that followed the completion of the six days of work. Cessation of the work of creation upon its completion in six days is hardly to be understood as God's twenty-four hour rest period. The response of Jesus to those who accused him of breaking the sabbath that was made for man, was, "My father worketh hitherto and I work" (John 15:17). Here Christ is indicating that both the Father and the Son have broken their creative rest day by working since the beginning. A triune God has entered into time with the work of mankind's redemption. This sabbath day's work will last until the heavens and earth, now under the curse, give way to new heavens and a new earth under the blessing of God. Man cannot measure this time. In this sense God's broken day of rest encompasses all of man's time. God's broken sabbath day becomes man's day of grace.

Time and the Ages of the Patriarchs

The ages of men given in Genesis have been problematical to the scientific mind. First, the life span of man from Adam to Noah is over ten times the present normal life expectancy. Second, the father-son sequence in which the ages of these men are given would place the time of the first man, Adam, at a much more recent date than many are inclined to accept. Estimates of time from Adam to the present based on the Biblical chronology of these men's ages, range from 6,000 to 10,000 years. These problems have received the attention of many writers. Yet, many readers are still looking for convincing answers and may be expecting such an attempt from this chapter. At the risk of being disappointing, the focus of our attention is on some questions that are seldom, if ever, asked.

The first of these questions is, "Why are the ages of Adam through Seth to Noah given, while the ages are not given for Cain and his descendants?" Very little is recorded in the Bible about the descendants of Adam through Seth other than their ages. For each one of these men we are given:

(1) their name
(2) the fact of their birth (except Adam)
(3) how long they lived before they begat the son that continued the geneology
(4) how long they lived after they begat this son
(5) the total number of years of their life
(6) their death (except Enoch who was translated)

In addition to these facts given regarding each patriarch the following brief remarks are made:

(1) To Seth also a son was born and he called his name Enos. At that time man began to call on the name of the Lord [or be called by the name of the Lord] (Genesis 4:26).
(2) Enoch walked with God; and He was not, for God took him (Genesis 4:24).
(3) When Lamech had lived an hundred and eighty-two years, he became the father of a son, and called his name Noah,

saying, Out of the ground which the Lord has cursed this one shall bring us relief from our work and from the toil of our hands (Genesis 4:28, 29).

In connection with Seth's naming of this son it is said that men began to be called by the name of the Lord. The line of Seth is thus identified as a line of witnesses. Their identification with the name of God is put before any political or religious identification. Enoch's translation is a witness to God's plan and faithfulness to enable man to walk with Him through life and of his final victory over death. Noah's testimony is to the judgment by water upon a sin-cursed earth.

There is no reason to doubt that the names of all of these men were in some way related to their witness. Both their names and their being known by the name of God were witnesses of God's righteousness and grace to the antediluvian world. The meanings of their names are as follows:

Adam	man
Seth	compensation, appointed
Enos	man, or mortal
Cainan	fixed
Mahalaleel	praise of God
Jared	descent
Enoch	initiated
Methuselah	man of the dart (said by some to mean, "at his death the sending forth of the waters")
Lamech	vigorous
Noah	rest, quiet

The death of each of these witnesses is mentioned, while that of Cain and his descendants is not. This fact calls to mind Psalm 116:15, "Precious in the sight of the Lord is the death of His saints."

In contrast to the line of witnesses, the ages of Cain and his descendants are not given. However, they are credited with developing the elements of a socio-political order that has all the marks of civilization. While no mention is made of writing, this does not necessarily mean that they had not developed such a system. Agriculture is associated with Cain who was a tiller of the soil. In contrast to Seth with whose son men began to be called by the name of the Lord, Cain built a city and named it after his son, Enoch. Lamech, the descendant of Cain, took two wives.

Jabal, his son by Adah, dwelt in tents and had cattle which indicates the development of animal husbandry. Jubal, the brother
of Jabal, was the father of those who played the lyre and the pipe.
These "non-percussion" wind and string instruments indicate the
cultural development of the fine arts, specifically music.

Tubal-Cain was the son of Lamech's other wife, Zillah. He was
a forger of all instruments of brass and iron. All of these activities
are elements of the complex cultural development called civilization.

The fact that no time is mentioned in relation to Cain's civilization is even more significant when we consider that every social
order that is known to man is built on some kind of time perspective. Many primitive peoples such as the tribes of the great
plains perceived their world as being without beginning. Their
past is a mythical past which never passes away, but which is the
basis for the present reality of their tribal existence. Through
their mythology, the ancient civilizations of Sumer and Egypt
perceived as inseparable the creation of their gods, their world
and their system of government.

Western man attempts to write history, rather than mythology, in
which time is a framework for understanding the relationships and
sequences of human events regarded as important to his social order. Yet, in Genesis the only relation of time to the social order
was the ages of the lives of those who were witnesses of God's
message to that antediluvian civilization.

What has been observed of the antediluvian patriarchs is also
true after the flood. The descendants of Shem, Ham, and Japheth
are given in Genesis 10. They are identified by their division into
lands, languages, families and nations, but no mention is made of
the length of their lives. The geneology for Shem leads down to
Eber and, his two sons, Peleg and Joktan. The descendants of Joktan
are then given in terms of geographic, linguistic, and political
divisions. Peleg, Joktan's brother, is merely mentioned as the witness
of an event, i.e., "for in his days the earth was divided" (Genesis
10:25). No socio-political location is given for Peleg or his descendants.

In Genesis 11 the geneology of Shem is repeated with ages given
from Shem to Abraham. No mention is made of Joktan and the
lineage is continued through Peleg. Again the ages of the builders
of civilizations and socio-political orders are not given, while those
men leading to Abram and eventually to Christ, are not politi-
cally identified but their ages are recorded.

This is not to say that those who only have the length of their
lives and their death recorded were isolated barbarians or inactive

parasites of society. What was pre-eminent in their lives was that they placed God first. This is clearly seen in the narrative of Cain and Abel. Abel had chosen first to be a keeper of sheep. Within the framework of Genesis, man had not yet been given animals to eat. Sheep were not a means of livelihood but were used for sacrifice and for the clothing of man's nakedness (Genesis 3:20). Abel placed the matter of his acceptance by God and his spiritual need first. Cain sought first his own material needs and had a little left over for God. God smiled on Abel's offering and refused Cain's.

Abel, no doubt, became a tiller of the soil, for he was in the field with Cain when his brother killed him. We are not told what part the descendants of Adam through Seth to Noah had in the antediluvian civilization. What we may be sure of, is that their involvement was a witness to God's presence and priority of His claims in the affairs of man. They sought first the kingdom of God and his righteousness.

If the Scriptures were written by holy men as they were moved by the Holy Spirit, then we may have here a time perspective that is not cultural — ancient or modern. Rather, there is presented the importance of time from the perspective of God and his redemptive efforts to enter the human temporal realm.

God's time perspective as expressed here in Genesis is in harmony with that which is explicitly recorded in II Peter 3:3-10.

> Knowing this first, that there shall come in the last days scoffers, walking after their own lusts, And saying, Where is the promise of his coming? for since the fathers fell asleep, all things continue as they were from the beginning of the creation. For this they willingly are ignorant of, that by the word of God the heavens were of old, and the earth standing out of the water and in the water: Whereby the world that then was, being overflowed with water, perished: But the heavens and the earth which are now, by the same word are kept in store, reserved unto fire against the day of judgment and perdition of ungodly men. But, beloved, be not ignorant of this one thing, that one day is with the Lord as a thousand years, and a thousand years as one day. The Lord is not slack concerning his promise, as some men count slackness; but is longsuffering to us-ward, not willing that any should perish, but that all should come to repentance. But the day of the Lord will come as a thief in the night; in the which the heavens shall pass away with a great noise, and the elements shall melt with fervent heat, the earth also and the works that are therein shall be burned up.

Time, from God's perspective, is a matter of grace. It is measured by the lives of witnesses. It is not measured by technological

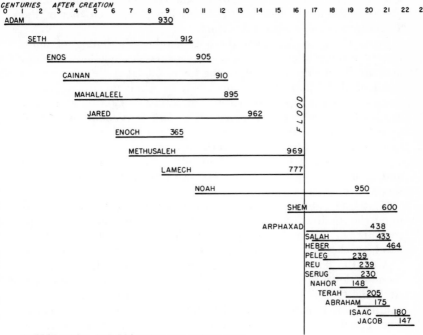

ANTEDILUVIAN AND POSTDILUVIAN PATRIARCHS
MASORETIC TEXT

FIGURE 8

instruments. It is not the framework of a cultural perspective nor the temporal structure of a social system.

A brief look at a chart of the ages of these patriarchs presents us with both a pattern and a problem.[1] With the exception of Enoch who was translated and Lamech who died just before the flood at 777 years, the length of lives from Adam to Noah is in a range from 895 to 969 years averaging a little over 900 years. Those living after the flood to Peleg range from 433 years to 464 years or a little less than half the life of those before the flood. Shem

---

[1] The Hebrew text is here chosen as the most reliable. According to the International Standard Bible Encyclopedia, "The general superiority of the Hebrew text of the Pentateuch as a whole to the Samaritan text and the Septuagint is no longer questioned by Biblical scholars." The difference in these texts is of greater concern to those who are using these ages to measure the chronology, than it is to the ideas presented in this article.

lived 600 years. He was born before the flood but lived most of his
life after the flood. The length of his life is between that of the
antediluvians and the post-diluvians.

From Peleg to Abraham there is another shortening of ages.
Here is a range from 148 to 239 years, or roughly one-half the ages
of those before the building of the tower of Babel.

All of these patriarchs from Adam to Abraham are a line of
witnesses. Their ages tell of the significance of God entering into
the limited time world of man in His work of redemption. There
appears to be a pattern of decrease in ages which also speaks of
God's entry into the temporal world of man.

After man's sin, God entered in by placing a curse upon man
and upon his environment, but He also provided a promise and a
sacrifice for man's redemption.

Next God entered the world through nature by sending a flood
upon the civilization that had rejected His word and promise of
redemption. The judgment in the garden and the judgment at the
flood, bracket the life span which is roughly a little over 900 years.

After the flood God entered the world of man a third time by
"coming down to see" the tower and the city that man was building.
At Babel God entered the cultural linguistic world of man by the
confusion of tongues. This led to their dispersion over the earth.
The Flood and the Tower of Babel bracket a time when the
ages of the witnesses average less than half of the ages of those before the flood, or over 400 years.

With the call and the covenant of Abraham, God enters the
world of human society with His unique plan to call men out and
make them witnesses of His covenant and lordship. Between the
confusion of tongues at Babel and God's covenant to Abraham,
Isaac, and Jacob, the age span becomes further shortened by about
one-half. The range of the lives of these men is from 239 years to
147 years. From the call and covenant of Abraham to the present
age, life expectancy is cut in half again — to the psalmist's three
score years and ten. The promise and covenant made to Abraham
finds its fulfillment in Jesus Christ, the climax of which will be His
return to make His enemies His footstool. With this event, time
as a day of grace for man, will come to an end.

The problem with which this chapter ends is presented by the
observation of the graph. The lives of many of these patriarchs
overlap, but Scripture does not in any wise refer to them as contemporaries. Before the flood, Noah is the only person who did not
live as a contemporary with Adam. Noah's death does not occur
until after the death of Peleg which would indicate that Noah was
living during the building of the tower of Babel and the confusing

of languages. Arphaxad, Salah, Peleg, Reu, Serug, Nahor, Terah, and Abraham all lived and died before the death of Shem, the son of Noah. And yet, of Abraham's death Scripture states, "These are the days of the years of Abraham's life which he lived, an hundred three score and fifteen years. Then Abraham gave up the ghost, and died in a good old age, an old man, and full of years; and was gathered to his people" (Genesis 25:7, 8). This statement is difficult to understand if Shem (who would have been over 500 years old) was still living. Abraham lived part of his life as a contemporary of Noah. Both Isaac and Jacob were born and lived some time as contemporaries with Shem.

In the Scripture, reference to these men is never as contemporaries and it would seem unlikely that they were. It is possible that we have no way of extending our modern concept of time beyond the cultural screen presented by the confusion of tongues at Babel. What seems here to be a time barrier in studies of Bible history is also a barrier in archeological studies of early civilization in this geographical area. Peoples who came into the Mesopotamian Valley and into the Nile Valley and into the Idus Valley, came as bearers of highly developed civilization. The past history of the development of these peoples and from whence they came, either eludes the archeologist's spade or is lost in his assumptions.

Conclusion

I do not think it would be unfounded speculation to grant the possibility that man's life span was greater in past ages than it is today. As great a catastrophe as is presented by the Biblical flood could not be an isolated phenomenon in the world of nature. It could well be associated with many other occurrences among which could be the shortening of the life expectancy of man. The additional factor that it was God's judgmental entrance into the realm of nature raises a number of questions among which are:

(1) Are all catastrophic events special expressions of divine anger? If not —
(2) Are there observable differences between natural and supernatural catastrophic events in nature?
(3) Can past supernatural events in nature be confirmed within the framework of natural science?

Other chapters in this symposium may be devoted to problems in these areas. This chapter has not assumed any burden of cause and effect explanations. We have not intended to say that the confusion of tongues at Babel cut man's life span in half. Nor has it been implied that God's covenant with Abraham resulted in the cutting of man's life span to the present three score years and ten. Without entering into any Biblical criticism a pattern has been observed in the ages of the patriarchs before and after the flood. This pattern has a message for modern man whether or not he is able historically or scientifically to explain it.

Genesis becomes an increasingly meaningful book when the Creator and Redeemer revealed therein is made known to the individual. The days of creation become a foundation for faith rather than a measurement by human mentality. They support the faith through which "we understand that the worlds were framed by the word of God, so that things which are seen were not made of things which do appear." The ages of the patriarchs give assurance that God has entered man's world of time and sense. They testify that the *true* measure of life's values is in the opportunity that time gives to receive the grace of God and to bear witness to it.

The Mythological Character
of Evolution

C. E. Allan Turner

C. E. ALLAN TURNER

C. E. Allan Turner was born in Hampshire, England in 1907. His education was received at Havant High School, Southampton University College and the University of London. He holds a B.S. (chemistry, 1929), M.Sc. (education, 1948), and the Ph.D. (education, 1952). His doctoral thesis was entitled "The Puritan Contributions to Scientific Education in the 17th Century in England."

Mr. Turner is a resident at Walton-on-Thames. He is currently master-in-charge of the Department of Religious Education at Surbiton Grammar School. He is an elder of a free church and a lay preacher. He is author of a number of pamphlets favoring creation and critical of evolution. He is also Chairman of the Evolution Protest Movement in England.

VI

THE MYTHOLOGICAL CHARACTER OF EVOLUTION

The scientific study of the Theory of Evolution requires as prerequisites definitions of both science and evolution. Sir Julian Huxley, F.R.S., a leading advocate of this theory, defines science as "the whole of organised and tested knowledge." So factual knowledge becomes the criterion in examining the idea of evolution. To be soundly scientific the theory must be based on facts, be in accord with all biological knowledge and be able to stand any test.

The term "evolution" is elusive of definition, being variously taken to mean development, growth, invention, variation, transformation. Charles Darwin did not give an exact definition, but W. R. Thompson, F.R.S., considers him as thinking "that all organisms that exist or have existed have developed from a few extremely simple forms of life or from one alone, by a process of descent by modification."[1] It is regarded as a process in which lifeless matter acted upon by chance through natural physical forces produced living organisms, from which through the course of millions or billions of years all living and extinct plants and animals, including man, developed.[2]

Reference to possibilities, or hopes, or biologists' prophecies are hardly scientific attitudes, but they are characteristic of Darwinism. Probabilities are not certainties, for if the statistical argument is to stand it must make an appeal to reality, that is, to a genuine sample which alone can give it validity. Statistics do not support the theory, as C. E. Guye, the Swiss mathematician, has demonstrated in calculating the chances of manufacturing a single molecule of some protein-like substance. While the odds are 10^{160} to 1 against the chance, the requirement of material needed for chance to synthesise a molecule is larger than the universe and the required time of 10^{243} years. This is obviously impossible if the age of the earth has been supposed at only 4×10^9 years. Further, Professor Leathes has calculated that the links in the chain of a protein could be combined in 10^{48} ways. Seeing the earth has been re-

---

[1]Introduction to *The Origin of Species*, Charles Darwin, J. M. Dent & Son, London, 1956. Evolution Protest Movement reprint, 1967, p. 6.

[2]*Evolution*, International Christian Crusade, Toronto, 1965, p. 7.

garded as cool enough for life for about 10^{15} seconds, chance would have to operate toward hypothetical synthesis at 10^{33} times per second to succeed![3] As C. H. Waddington, F.R.S. of Edinburgh University wrote:

> Have we not tended to over-emphasise the importance of chance processes in evolution?

Again,

> Something more than chance must have been at work.[4]

The alleged rate of laying down of the geological strata presupposes a uniformitarianism which is neither demonstrable nor in accord with known facts. Apart from the Creator being considered as a directing or intervening Intelligence, the earth has been subjected in the past to numerous catastrophes from outer space such as gravitational interactions — tides — of planetary dimensions, and meteoric collisions accompanied by tidal waves and from within in the nature of earthquakes and eruptions. These powerful forces produce major effects in a minimum time. The possibility of varying radiation, too, as a factor of change cannot be scientifically excluded.

Refuge being taken by evolutionists in long periods of time as necessary to produce evolutionary changes may well be ludicrous wishful thinking. Time itself changes nothing. The continued existence of living oysters like their fellows sometime ago fossilized in Portland stone or of such creatures as the diatom Navicula Lyra[5] in the Delaware River, but also found as a fossil of a supposed thirty-five million years' standing in Moravia shows how immune they are to this fiction. Similarly, the Coelacanth, a fish with fins jointed like arms, was regarded as an intermediate, which became extinct a supposed sixty million years ago. It left numerous fossils, but in 1938, in 1952, and since, live specimens have been taken from the sea off Madagascar. (At the same time it should be noted that here was no intermediate.) It is a definite fish, complete with gills, scales and fins, incapable of living in shallow water, and thus most unlike any supposed amphibian link. G. G. Simpson, himself an evolutionist of note, states none of the animal

---

[3]F. W. Cousins, Evolution Protest Movement Pamphlet No. 164.
[4]*Nature of Life*, 1961.
[5]F. W. Cousins, *Diatoms*, E.P.M. Pamphlet No. 99.

phyla have become extinct and that the major grades of organisation appear to be nearly immortal.[6]

The Theory as a matter for scientific inquiry strictly rules itself out of court on two counts. First, it appears to be dependent on events which occurred in the remote past, unobserved and unobservable — a historical process, requiring historical evidence, itself dependent on human testimony, obviously not forthcoming. Also, it is described as a process, but again it is unobservable as such. Fossils are like a series of still pictures which suggest a story that may deceive a cinema audience, but film makers know that behind the scenes they are disconnected "shots," often made far apart in time and place.

If refuge is taken in the statement that changes are very gradual and occur over long periods of time, then the probability is that intermediates will be numerous and finely-graded, which happens not to be the case. The Theory propounded by Darwin over a century ago still lacks proof. His confidence that when the geologic record would be completed numerous intermediates would be found, has not been fulfilled. Indeed, evolutionists have admitted that three-quarters of the evidence is lacking.

> That evolution actually did occur can only be scientifically established by the fossilised remains of representative samples of those intermediate types which have been postulated on the basis of the indirect evidence. In other words, the really crucial evidence for evolution must be provided by the paleontologist whose business it is to study the fossil record.[7]

Yet Heribert Nilsson, former Director of the Botanical Institute, Lund, Sweden, states:

> The fossil material is now so complete that . . . the lack of transitional series cannot be explained as due to scarcity of material. *The deficiencies are real, they will never be filled.*[8]

G. G. Simpson, of New York, also states that paleontological investigations have been unable to discover transitional forms leading to thirty-two orders of mammals. Further, he writes,

> This regular absence of transitional forms is not confined to mammals, but is an almost universal phenomenon as has long been

---

[6]*Tempo and Mode in Evolution*, Columbia University Press, New York, 1944, p. 113.
[7]*Discovery*, January, 1955, p. 7.
[8]*Synthetische Artbildung*, C. W. K. Gleerup, 1953, p. 1212.

noted by paleontologists. It is true of almost all classes of animals, both vertebrate and invertebrate.[9]

And this is after frantic search for evidence in the field and laboratory with every device over a period of a hundred years.

The evolutionists' sublime dependence on "Natural Selection" to account for evolution suggests a personalized power rather than a scientific term capable of definition, while acting in predictable ways from and on physical entities. Nor can it (Natural Selection) be an agent like a farmer choosing seeds or bulls for breeding. It may be noted that the emphasis on this "selector" has been much reduced in recent years by such biologists as Cannon, Haldane, and Good. Also, Kenneth W. Cooper, of the University of Rochester, points out how unscientific is the method employed:

> As is so often the case in the writings of our modern evolutionists, natural selection as a cause is deduced from effect, and the resulting arguments and conclusions are, of course, unconvincing.[10]

The concept of species has varied from time to time. Some have suggested that differences between species are not well marked, while other workers, such as Ernst Mayr, state that species are not agglomerations of various mutations or variant individuals, but are "integrated and cohesive genepools, homeostatic and change-resistant."[11] H. Nilsson has described a species as a "sphere of variation" and the supreme unit in nature, which is constant, the number and nature of the variants being limited to the possibilities of different combinations of the genes.[12] R. Goldschmidt, of the University of California, suggests that:

> It is good to keep in mind . . . that nobody has ever succeeded in producing a new species, not to mention the higher categories, by selection of micro-mutations.[13]

Inbreeding between true species even if supposedly closely related results in sterile offspring. While the horse and ass mate to produce the infertile mule, the cat cannot interbreed with the lynx. In the wild, species do not normally interbreed, so Nilsson observes:

> Nature sweeps clean the border lines of the species.

---

[9]"Tempo and Mode in Evolution," Columbia University Press, New York, p. 106.
[10]Science, March 25, 1955, p. 429.
[11]Huxley, Nature, August 31, 1963, p. 839.
[12]Op cit., p. 1176.
[13]Theoretical Genetics, University of California Press, 1955, p. 488.

The production, or "re-creation" of animals long extinct, effected by Hans Heck,[14] of Munich Zoo, is like evolution in reverse. Thus the breeding of the aurioch or wild ox of Europe, extinct for 300 years, was effected by crossing of the Corsican semi-wild cattle with fighting bulls from France. The tarpans or ancient wild horses were obtained by crossing a wild Mongolian stallion with mares from Iceland and Gotland. Such experiments show no new species have been obtained in modern times but that the new types have been produced by a manipulation of existing pools of genes. They may also suggest that living species would, if left to themselves, soon revert to a few primitive types.

Mere assertions that evolution is a "law," statements that biologists believe it and the erection of fragile towers of hypotheses based on hypotheses are no substitutes for proof. As knowledge has increased, crude suggestions of intermediates such as whales between mammals and fish, or bats, or the platypus between birds and mammals, have been dropped. Such suggestions, as coming down heavily on one side as undoubted mammals, yet needing the support of other creatures, are still markedly dubious.

The three fossils of Archeopteryx found in Germany have been hailed in the text books as the best example of a link, this time between birds and reptiles. A detailed examination has shown this to be an undoubted bird with feathers and beak. The score from the writings of even the evolutionary biologists is 37 to 8 in favor of the classification as bird.[15] Moreover, today there lives in the woods and swamps of the Amazon valley the Hoactzin or Anna bird. This is similar in size and structure to Archaeopteryx, which is supposed to have had similar habits.

It is interesting to note, however, that G. G. Simpson does not mention Archeopteryx in his book, *The Meaning of Evolution.* More careful than most of his fellow evolutionists, did he have it in mind in referring to types between reptiles and birds, and yet regard it of less value as evidence? Contrary to the earlier view, recent work suggests that feathers of birds cannot be regarded as developed from frayed epidermis of reptiles or intermediates as they belong to a different layer of skin.

Another piece of alleged evidence for evolution, cited in many textbooks, is the supposed ancestry of the horse. This has been hailed as particularly valuable, as some twenty different fossils have been named as intermediates. The Greek prefixes to *hippus* namely, *eo, oro, meso, mio, para, mery, proto, plesi,* have been used

---

[14]*London Illustrated News*, March 19, 1949, p. 381.
[15]See author's *Archaeopteryx*, E.P.M. Pamphlet No. 76.

to name them, and conveniently suggest the conclusions to be drawn that they are intermediates. Other ideas such as their being variants from the existing stock or entirely different creatures have again been conveniently rejected. However, among the evolutionists there is hardly scientific unanimity as D. Dewar[16] shows the order of these fossils is largely guesswork since over twenty different pedigrees have been suggested. Further confusion is seen in conflicting theories as to how fossils in widely separated countries can be related. For the supposed earliest (*eohippus*) appear in Asia, while in England and France a number appear in the same stratum (Lower Eocene) as do their alleged ancestors in Wyoming.

Then after all the investigation it must be remembered that this represents only an alleged case of evolution within a family, not the development of a new order. But should the evolutionists be convinced that the modern horse is descended from *eohippus*, they have lost their case. For, if that creature existed sixty million years ago according to their supposition, then it would take ten times longer for a new order to develop and then ten times that for a new class making altogether six thousand million years. This would then leave no time for evolution from the simplest forms of life, as that is the evolutionist's estimated age of the earth.[17]

There has been a feverish hunt through the century for evidence of man's ancestry. So anxious have the seekers been to obtain results that H. Woollard, of London, as long ago as 1938, criticised their methods in these terms:

> When a new fossil has been discovered, the discoverer has been unable to resist the temptation of asserting that his fossil, if ape-like, presented all sorts of human characteristics, and if human and clearly modern in character, that it is possessed of all sorts of simian characters more or less hidden and elucidated only by minute examination.

He concludes as an evolutionist:

> The notion of the gradual emergence of man seems the more reasonable, and has exerted a seductive influence upon the minds of anatomists.[18]

An early supposed link was the Neanderthal Man, with massive facial features, but the numerous fossils have shown a large

---

[16]*The Transformist Illusion*, 1955, p. 90.
[17]For fuller discussion see:
  Dewar, D., *The Transformist Illusion*, and the author's *Horse Sense about Horse Evolution*, E.P.M. Pamphlet No. 74.
[18]*Science Progress*, July, 1938.

brain and no simian characters, leaving it as representing an extinct race of man. Thus, like many other such cases, it comes down heavily on one side of the gap.

Eugene Dubois journeyed from Holland to Sumatra to discover the missing link. This, he alleged, he had found when he returned in 1895 with an ape-like skull cap and a human femur together making such a creature. What he did not then reveal was that he found the latter fifty feet away, and a year later, and that he had unearthed four more such femurs and a human tooth at the same place. He disclosed this in 1930, and eventually announced his link was a giant gibbon with half the brain capacity of man.[19] But this Java Man or Pithecanthropus was supposed to be a link.

At Piltdown, Sussex, in 1912, a simian jaw and bones from the dome of a human skull were found, to be hailed as Eoanthropus or the Piltdown "dawn" man 500,000 years old. This was the verdict of the experts of the day, namely: Sir Arthur Smith Woodward, Sir Ray Lankester, Sir Grafton Elliot Smith, F.R.S., and, later, Sir Arthur Keith. However, by 1953 the union of the bones was declared a forgery of a recent chimpanzee jaw and a 50,000-year-old human skull.[20] By 1959 the skull was declared only 500 years old.

On the other side of the Atlantic, in 1922, Henry Fairfield Osborn, head of the American Museum of Natural History, found in a Pliocene deposit of Nebraska, a single molar tooth. This was hailed as the first American: "Hesperopithecus." Sir Grafton Elliot Smith had drawings of the male and female of this specimen, based on one tooth, published in the *London Illustrated News* of June 24, 1922. However, the link disappeared five years later as being part of an extinct peccary (or pig).

In caves near Peking, Davidson Black and J. G. Anderssen discovered, in 1921, bones which became known as the Peking Man or Sinanthropus pekinensis. Abbé N. Breuil, in 1932, after inspecting the caves, concluded that the numerous bones found there were of large apes killed by man for food and thrown into the huge furnaces which had existed in the caves.

Another such find was the fossil, Proconsul Africanus, discovered in 1926 and hailed as an ape-man, but discredited in 1958 as being a primitive anthropoid ape, after the finding of the bones of his hand and forearm.[21] So much again, for the value of the "links."

These examples of discredited links are only part of the un-

---

[19]A. G. Tilney, *Pithecanthropus: The Facts*, E.P.M. Pamphlet No. 75.
[20]Francis Vere, *Lessons of Piltdown*, E.P.M. 1959.
[21]*Time*, July 28, 1958, p. 46.

scientific confusion that exists over attempts to find man's ancestors. There is also the unfair rejection of the Castenedolo and Olmo skulls found in Pliocene deposits in Italy and the Calaveras skull from the same stratum in California. This is because they are of modern types and would show man on the evolutionist's reasoning to be older than his alleged apelike ancestors! And there are other such fossils, including the Foxhall and Swanscombe, which pose similar problems.

Much of the support of the theory of evolution is derived from the mischievous theory of the existence of the Geological Column. This supposes fossils to have existed in an orderly sequence in successive strata, showing how one has developed into others. Such is quite contrary to the facts. First it should be noted that the order of the strata (as some are reversed) and their identification, are matters of debate. Only a few are found in any one area and many are missing from various parts of the earth. Like Heribert Nilsson, V. H. Heywood states:

> Good fossil sequences are known for very few groups, and for many there seems little likelihood of their ever becoming available.[22]

Then it is to be noted that no indubitable fossils are found below the Cambrian rocks, above which they occur suddenly and continue in profusion.

In *The Fossil Record*, of the Geological Society of London, and the Palaeontological Association, 1967,[23] the charts show this and that the Protozoa (single-celled) occur after the Metazoa (many-celled), for Molluscs and foot-long Triolites appear as the earliest forms. This is at least honest, but contrary to evolutionary theory.

The book shows no intermediates between fishes and amphibians, the amphibians and reptiles, or between reptiles and mammals in Chapters 26, 27, 28, and 30. The series of fossil horses of dubious validity gives no indication of linkage with other orders of mammals. Also no evidence of evolution is seen among the plants, as Angio-sperms (flowering plants) appear all at once and in great diversity; the dicots and the monocots also appear together.

The publication gives a fabrication to the fanciful genealogical "trees" of animals and plants which adorn text books. E. A. Hooton, in the revised edition of his book *Up from the Ape*, 1958, follow-

---

[22]*Times Science Review*, Summer, 1964, p. 12.
[23]Reviewed in E.P.M. Pamphlet No. 162.

ing the Piltdown exposure, retains Eoanthropus as being a necessary, if now only imagined, part of his tree. He begs his readers
not to take the efforts at primate arboriculture too seriously! Yet,
this is continuing the practice of the earlier evolutionists. E. A.
Haeckel, professor of Zoology at Jena, 1862-1909, fanatical, reck-
less and unscrupulous, falsified human embryo sketches to bolster
the theory, as he was finally forced to admit.[24] Similarly, T. H.
Huxley, 1825-1895, although he declared the theory unproven, in
his drawings of skeletons placed more emphasis on similarities
between apes and men than on their differences, and showed apes
upright and man not completely so.[25]

At the Symposium of the Systematics Association at Liverpool,
in 1964, systems of classification and genealogical trees, based on
the theory of evolution without adequate support, were criticized
by the opening speaker, V. H. Heywood.[26] Similarly, W. R. Thompson, F.R.S., states:

> Taxonomists also followed the trend, constructing hypothetical
> ancestors for their groups and explaining the derivation of existing
> forms from these imaginary entities.[27]

The tendency to produce fiction in the name of science continues since Haeckel's time. The Nebraska tooth above was re-
habilitated into the prehistoric American *and his wife and contemporary animals* in the double (folio) page picture printed in
the *London Illustrated News* of June 24, 1922, by Sir Grafton
Elliot Smith, F.R.S. The four hundred fragments of the skull of
Zinanthropus Boisei, discovered by Mary Leakey, in 1959, has
been "clothed" with flesh and hair by three different artists in
pictures published for "scientific" articles. These would suggest
there were three entirely different and unrelated creatures — so
much for scientific exactitude.[28]

E. Dubois produced a complete model, still residing in the vaults
of Leiden Museum of his pseudo-link, Pithecanthropus Erectus.
The British Museum, in its official publication *Evolution*, 1959,
has used the pictures by Maurice Wilson to depict the part skull
of Australopithecus as a whole man, as well as those of the Peking
man and others. Such activities neither help the theory nor
honor science except in the eyes of the ignorant and the credulous.

---

[24]Assmuth, J. and Hull, E. R., *Haeckel's Frauds and Forgeries*, 1915.
[25]Huxley, Weidenriech, *Apes, Giants, and Man*, pp. 6-7.
[26]*Nature*, September 19, 1964.
[27]*Introduction*, p. 16.
[28]The author, *Fictional Reconstructions*, E.P.M. Pamphlet No. 151.

The words of the late Wood Jones, of the Royal College of Surgeons, England, regarding the so-called reconstruction of supposed human ancestors, were:

> I find no occupation less worthy of the science of anthropology than the now unfashionable business of modelling, painting and drawing these nightmare pictures of imagination, and lending them in the process an utterly false value of apparent reality.[29]

And this unworthy occupation is still being followed nearly forty years later.

The anatomical examination of mammals was supposed to give support to the theory. Wiedersheim, quoted by J. H. Huxley and H. G. Wells, enumerated some 180 vestigial organs, wholly or almost useless in man, but useful in various species of animals.[30] This number has since been reduced to about six, namely, the appendix, the coccyx, the plica semilunaris, the pineal gland, the muscles of the outer ear, and the tonsils. The fact that the removal of such organs without serious disabilities resulting does not mean they are useless anymore than a lost eye or arm. However, for each of these organs, following further research, useful functions have been found. The appendix and the tonsils, for example, serve as protective organs, while the coccyx gives support to eliminatory muscles, and viscera.[31] So these are not vestiges from evolving ancestors, but valuable aids for present living.

With reference to so-called rudiments such as the homologues of the mammary glands in a man, they can hardly be regarded as vestiges of organs which were at one time functional whatever their present use.[32] Also, the late Rendle Short, former professor of surgery, at Bristol, points out that the Darwinian tubercle on the human ear and the multiple nipples are hardly evidence of man's simian ancestry, as no ape has pointed ears or multiple nipples.[33]

Embryology was also called upon to provide evidence for evolution. The hypothesis, that each species recapitulates its stages of evolutionary development, was called Haeckel's "Biogenetic Law," and supported by his discredited drawings. The amniotic fluid in which embryos lie in the womb is very different from any possible primitive sea in which life was supposed to have begun. Further,

---

[29]*Man's Place Among the Mammals*, Longmans, Green & Co., 1929, p. 66.
[30]*The Science of Life*, Vol. 1, Doubleday, Doran & Co., 1931, p. 415.
[31]For further discussion see John R. Howitt, *Evolution*, 1965, pp. 29-33.
[32]Thompson, *Introduction*, p. 11.
[33]Transactions of the Victoria Institute, 1935, p. 256.

the embryo derives its food from the mother through the umbilical cord and not from this liquid. Also, there is no question of the embryo respiring by gills to extract oxygen from the fluid. Supposed gill-slits in the embryo have been shown to be no more than cervical folds with no perforations.

The circulatory system is supposed to have started as a simple duct, part of which developed into a heart. Yet in the embryo the heart develops before the blood vessels. Sir Gavin deBeer states that teeth were developed before tongues, but now in mammals tongues came before teeth. Thus, evolutionary mythology would predict exactly the reverse order of prenatal development to that which actually occurs.

The late A. Rendle Short has stated regarding deformities occurring in newborn infants, such as cleft palate, club foot, spina bifida, supernumerary fingers or toes, or webbed fingers, that they:

> are in no way characteristic of any possible ancestor. The statement is often copied from book to book that babies may be born with a tail. It is safe to say that of a thousand babies *with* congenital malformations, not more than one will show the alleged tail, and when it does occur it will usually be a fatty or sacrococcygeal tumour, and quite unlike the tail of a monkey. Apes, of course, have no tail.[34]

That embryological evidence is valueless is shown in the statement of Waldo Shumway:

> There is never a time in the development of the mammal when it could be mistaken for a fish or a reptile.[35]

Further, the late Sir Arthur Keith said:

> Now that the appearances of the embryo at all stages are known, the general feeling is one of disappointment: the human embryo at no stage is anthropoid in its appearance.[36]

Attempts have been made to secure evidence of evolution occurring before our eyes rather than over many millennia. One case cited is that of black-backed gulls turning grey. Another is of melanism (blackening) occurring in the grey British Peppered moth, Biston betularia. This latter was supposed to be due to adaptation to smoky industrial conditions. What has not been

[34]*Modern Discovery and the Bible*, Inter Varsity Fellowship, 1952, p. 107.
[35]*Introduction to Vertebrate Embryology*, John Wiley and Sons, 4th Edition, 1949, p. 4.
[36]*The Human Body*, Thornton, Butterworth, 1932, p. 94.

disclosed in the argument is that the black forms occurred before the industrial era, and that they are ousting the grey in rural areas as well.[37] In any case, gulls remain gulls, and moths remain moths, no new species being formed.

Experiments to demonstrate evolution have been attempted in the laboratory. The best known and most extended, perhaps, has been the breeding of the fruit fly *Drysophila*. Hundreds of mutant forms have been produced by exposure to X-rays, but in each case the creature has been deformed rather than improved.[38] These forms are fertile when crossed with the original types and they remain the same species of the fruit fly. Similarly, irradiated mice produce "kinky" tails, which is hardly an advantage to the mouse or an important step in proving the evolution of the species. In any case, such agents as high level X-ray radiation at such strengths are quite artificial means of producing change.

Carl Lindegren, of Southern Illinois University, states:

> I am of the opinion that *progressive* evolution has never been observed in the laboratory.[39]

Also, H. Graham Cannon, of Manchester University, declares:

> No experiment has produced progeny that show entirely new functioning organs. And yet it is the appearance of new characters in organisms which marks the boundaries of the major steps in the evolutionary scales.[40]

So the scientific laboratory hardly helps the evolutionary cause.

The Second Law of Thermodynamics states that in all energy changes some of the energy tends to be transferred into non-reversible heat-energy. This is given in other words in the Law of Entropy, that, in a closed system, entropy increases, or the measure of availability of the energy of a system for the performance of work or maintenance of the life-process decreases.[41] This means decreasing organization is characteristic of the universe, which is thus approaching "heat-death." Now the idea of evolution

---

[37]E. B. Ford, F.R.S., *The Evolution of Life*, University of Chicago Press, 1960, p. 193.

[38]*Evolution*, p. 37.

[39]*Scientific American*, March, 1950, p. 2.

[40]*The Evolution of Living Things*, Manchester University Press, 1958, p. 92.

[41]E. H. Betts and C. E. A. Turner, *Entropy Disproves Evolution*, E.P.M. Pamphlet No. 62.

is completely contrary to this law of science, as the theory involves a continual increase in order, organization, size, and complexity. Elements pass from the reactive to a stable state. Organic matter left to itself in normal conditions decays. The molecules of compounds, such as proteins, which are essential to life, are complex organizations and break down readily. Also, they are not found separate in nature from living material. There is no spontaneous making of life. Where organic matter is formed it is catalyzed by matter produced by living organisms. The Kornberg experiment of producing a new DNA molecule was performed by using the appropriate enzymes. Here the enzymes needed for such processes are the products of the living cell. So Sir Cyril Hinshelwood, F.R.S., in his presidential address to the British Association for the Advancement of Science, states that:

> It would be fallacious to suppose that the major code-bearing molecules, the nucleic acids, can as a matter of pure structural chemistry, replicate themselves in isolation. They do so only in the integrated organisation of a living cell.[42]

The very complexity, order and precision in the structure and function of living creatures would be a scientific argument against evolution through chance. There is the complexity of such molecules as chlorophyll in the plant with its single magnesium atom exactly sited amid the thousands of other atoms. Blood contains haemogloben with an iron atom, again combined with thousands of others. Even the commonest proteins have a particular structure composed again of thousands of atoms. The single cell containing these and the even more complex DNA (deoxyribonucleic acid) molecule with its racial code in its nucleus functioning with other material, follows intricate procedures as it survives, reproduces and serves the larger organism. Again, each organism consists of many different types of cells, each with its specific function. All organisms in turn live as perfect, separate, independent units, ranging from insect to bird, hydra to whale, bat to elephant.

That the theory of evolution is poor science is perhaps best seen through the pronouncement of prominent scientists — themselves not all to be labelled creationists. The late William Bateson, F.R.S., of Cambridge University, well defined the crucial test in stating:

> Every theory of evolution must be such as to accord with the facts of physics and chemistry, a primary necessity to which our predecessors paid small heed.[43]

---

[42]*New Scientist*, September 2, 1965.
[43]*Nature*, August 20, 1914.

W. R. Thompson, F.R.S., points out:

> Darwin considered that the doctrine of the origin of living forms by
> descent with modification, even if well founded, would be unsatis-
> factory unless the causes at work were correctly identified.[44]

Further, he states:

> There is a great divergence of opinion among biologists, not only
> about the causes of evolution but even about the actual process.
> This divergence exists because the evidence is unsatisfactory and
> does not permit any certain conclusion. It is, therefore, right and
> proper to draw the attention of the non-scientific public to the dis-
> agreements about evolution. But some recent remarks of evolution-
> ists show that they think this is unreasonable. This situation,
> where scientific men rally to the defence of a doctrine they are
> unable to define scientifically, much less demonstrate with scien-
> tific rigor, attempting to maintain its credit with the public by the
> suppression of criticism and the elimination of difficulties, is ab-
> normal and undesirable in science.[45]

Earlier he had written:

> I am not satisfied that Darwin proved his point or that his in-
> fluence in scientific and public thinking has been beneficial.[46]

L. J. Stadler, of Yale University, has well said:

> As to the sources and mechanisms of the variations found in evolu-
> tion on the grand scale, the development of experimental genetics
> to date has placed little restriction upon free speculation. The
> investigation of time series, trends, and rates of evolution . . .
> necessarily remains today, as in Darwin's time, a wholly descrip-
> tive science.[47]

. . . or no science at all.

The weakness of the scientific case for evolution is illustrated
in the wriggling of its arch priest, Sir Julian Huxley, F.R.S. As
early as 1934 J. L. Russell said that he:

> appears to suffer, even more acutely than most popular scientists,
> from an inability to distinguish facts which have already been dis-
> covered from facts which he hopes will be discovered.[48]

---

[44]*Op. cit.*, p. 8.
[45]*Ibid*, p. 17.
[46]*Ibid*, p. 5.
[47]*Science*, April 21, 1950, p. 423.
[48]*Scrutiny*, Volume III, December 1934, p. 277.

Faced with the fact that evolution cannot be shown to be a continuing process, Huxley states:

> It seems probable that life's major trends have run their course.[49]

Again, we have his unscientific statement:

> In conclusion, we have the glorious paradox that this purposeless mechanism, after a thousand million years of its automatic operations, has finally created purpose — as one of the attributes of our own species.[50]

Later he explained that:

> Though natural selection is an ordering principle, it operates blindly . . . without conscious purpose or any awareness of an aim.[51]

On this Gertrude Himmelfarb remarks:

> Posing as a massive deduction from the evidence, it ends up as an ingenious argument from ignorance.[52]

It might also be said that any scientific principle such as gravity acts blindly, and for it to display "conscious purpose," it would need to be a personality!

Instead of glossing over ignorance, some scientists are prepared to admit it. So H. Hamshaw Thomas, F.R.S., of Cambridge University, states:

> The evolution of the flowering plants is probably as great a mystery as it was a century ago.[53]

His fellow botanist, J. Doyle, of Dublin University, in his Presidential Address to the Botany Section of the British Association for the Advancement of Science, 1957, said:

> Modern man may point with pride to his achievements in engineering and electronics — to television, electronic computers, supersonic planes, and the like. But he cannot even begin to conceive how he could make a single blade of grass. He obviously fails here because

---

[49]*Endeavor,* January, 1946, p. 12.
[50]Rationalist Annual, 1946, p. 87.
[51]*Evolution of Life,* University of Chicago Press, 1960, p. 20.
[52]*Darwin and the Darwinian Revolution,* Chatto and Windus, 1959, p. 276.
[53]*Nature,* December 15, 1956, p. 1314.

he knows too little of its form and nature. Since we cannot explain the everyday phenomena of onotogenic development, it seems to be just intellectual presumption to claim to offer a sort of blanket explanation of the global evolution of all animate nature over a thousand million years of geological time.[54]

Ronald Good, of Hull University, on the development of new forms, stated:

Above all there is the very reasonable and — dare I say it? — self-evident statement that no amount of selection alone can initiate novelty: and it is the origin of novelty, in the sense of the periodic appearance of conditions which have never before occurred, that must have been the fundamental theme of the evolutionary story. Such objections as these have never been met, though they have become blanketed in varying degrees by circumstances.[55]

He further states:

By the proper standards of scientific argument, evolution is not a fact.[56]

Earlier he wrote:

Although evolution finds wide tacit acceptance as a grand organising concept of biology and as the best working hypothesis, to explain the present multifariousness of plant and animal life, many people gravely doubt the validity of many of the more particular arguments by which it is customarily sustained. Some even question the whole idea. The biological sciences today are thus in the uneasy position of having to use, as one of their principal tools, a body of theory which is both sententious and incomplete, and one in which many workers have less than complete confidence.[57]

As Sir Cecil G. Wakeley, F.R.S.E., former President of the Royal College of Surgeons, England, observed:

It seems such a pity in a scientific age where precision and detail are so important that the vast majority of modern scientists believe in evolution, and yet the basic facts are against such a theory.

The theory, in conclusion, has all the appearance of nineteenth century mythology (anti-Biblical), of wishful thinking, of the desire

---

[54]*The Advancement of Science*, 54, September, 1957, p. 11.
[55]*Listener*, May 7, 1959, p. 797.
[56]*Ibid.*, June 6, 1959.
[57]*Bible League Quarterly*, Jan.-March, 1965, p. 194.

for a tidy process, for an easily-grasped pattern, excluding the Creator. It is the hypothesis founded on hypotheses, a mixture of fact and fiction, a block to biological research. It is the pursuit of a phantom force along a tenuous trail of yesteryear that never was. It garbs a ghost of unproven theory with a flimsy semblance of living reality. It uses the prestige of science to impress a belief, and is reasoning contrary to the scientific method of humble, careful and accurate investigation of the physical world. It is nineteenth century mythology wearing a mask of science appealing to that quality within each of us that would flee from both the knowledge as well as from the presence of our Creator.

Creation: The Only Reasonable Explanation of Natural Phenomena

W. Hewitt Tier

W. HEWITT TIER

Mr. Tier was born in Southampton, England, in 1886 and was educated at Portsmouth and at Reading University College where he held the position of associate. He later served as an educator in science fields in schools in England and New Zealand, the latter place where he was head master.

Mr. Tier's interest in creation and its evolutionary antithesis began at the age of 15, when the theory of evolution disturbed his belief in the truth of the Bible. Intensive and wide-ranging reading on the subject followed. This led to his deep and profound conclusion as to the majesty of creation, with its superior logic, and the falsity of the theory of evolution. His conclusions have motivated the writing of several articles and pamphlets for the Evolution Protest Movement and other publications. He has served the Evolution Protest Movement as a council member since 1956.

VII

CREATION: THE ONLY REASONABLE EXPLANATION OF NATURAL PHENOMENA

PART I

The Super-terrestrial

If the Bible is accepted to be a revelation from God about matters which concern mankind, but which do not come within the range of our finite powers of investigation and discovery: more precisely, if we believe that we are the subjects of a Supreme Being who is concerned for our present state and our eternal welfare, we shall find little difficulty in accepting the written statement by Moses, as God's mouthpiece, that "In the beginning God created the heavens and the earth" together with the formal record of how the flora and fauna came into existence. Those who do not accept the truth of Genesis I are reminded by the Apostle Paul that "the invisible things of him from the creation of the world are clearly seen, being understood by the things that are made, even his eternal power and Godhead" (Romans 1:20). This constitutes a challenge to human intelligence and reason which should be carefully noted, because it comes from a source which claims to transcend human reason, where this is necessary, for our fuller knowledge of God's purposes: e.g., Why should we expect divine mercy?

It is, no less, a challenge to true science as well as to that which the Bible calls "science so-called." The latter embraces conclusions based on incomplete or inadequate knowledge, imaginations, suppositions, and the like, which abound in the theory called Evolution. If the public were fully aware that so many of the statements by scientists are mere surmises, there might now be much to complain about. On the contrary, alas, these guesses are often presented as proven facts. We need only recall the case of the Piltdown Man, exposed within the last decade as a fraud. This is true also of the so-called Java Man, the Peking Man, and many other impositions on public credulity. These rash inventions are themselves evidence of the very shaky foundation of the theory they are seeking to uphold.

Extreme evolutionists often ridicule the idea of creation, and some are anxious to dismiss the Deity as a figment of the imagination. They presume to think that, given unlimited time, there is nothing that cannot be explained by the processes of nature. But not all their co-theorists are happy about such conclusions; nor are they all anti-God. Many Christians are very concerned to reconcile their religious beliefs with these supposed scientific facts and discoveries. These so-called Theistic Evolutionists imagine that the evidences of evolution are overwhelming. This is partly due to ignorance concerning natural phenomena; partly due to their inability to meet the scientist on his own ground; and, we must add, not less to the profundity of the many questions involved, some of which a lifetime of study could not solve. In truth, difficulties multiply as efforts are made to reconcile the Judao-Christian revelation with the Theory of Evolution and the theory itself with the evidence presented by natural phenomena.

Before turning to the more interesting and positive evidences of creation, we will suggest, for the reader's consideration, one or two of these difficulties. First, if God can create either one or any number of single-celled animalcule with such innate powers of development and variation as would be necessary for the furnishing of the earth as we see it, what objection can there be to the idea of God directly creating the flora and fauna? Are we, in consequence, to credit these animalculae with the power to produce man "in the image and likeness of God?" If we think it impossible that God could have created man in this way by a direct act why credit Him with the even more inscrutable power necessary in order to create these microscopic amoeba and confer on them such powers as to confound human understanding?

We are faced with a further problem. If we allow that God has the power to produce all the phenomena of nature by direct creation, both animate and inanimate, what reason, do we imagine, constrained Him to confuse the issue by relinquishing this mighty power and conferring it on the amoeba which, therefore, by ordinary reasoning processes, should make it an object of our worship? Of course, the non-theistic evolutionist regards it as a matter of chance and, if it comes to the point, the amoeba itself must exist by mere chance and be quite unaccountable in its existence.

We are told in Genesis I that God created the fauna, but we are not told that this was so with the flora. There is a notable passage in Genesis 2:4, 5, which reads:

> These are the generations of the heavens and the earth when they were created, in the day that the Lord God made the earth and the heavens, and every plant of the field before it was in the earth, and every herb of the field before it grew.

The suggestion here is that the terrestrial flora in all its variety was conceived in the mind of God before ever it was in the earth and was provided for, while the earth lasts, in the tiny seed from which the earth brought forth fruit in due time. The seed, under its appropriate conditions, produces the fully-developed plant. What God directly ordained transpires according to His will and provision. Evolutionists will find no support for their theory in these pronouncements.

Super-terrestrial Evidences of Creation

The Sun

The earth is not by any means a self-sustaining body. Its internal heat, whatever its explanation or origin, has no power to warm its surface. Nor is its illumination a product of its own chemical action or energy of any kind. It is a dependent body in all its distinctive characteristics. It is inherently desolate apart from external influences which act upon it: notably the sun, whose beneficial influence is contingent on many precise and delicate conditions providentially provided and maintained.

This heavenly body, which is ninety-three million miles away (approx.) from the earth, is at exactly the right distance to perform the countless miracles advantageous to our planet and the life it bears. This cannot be said of any other solar body. It is now recognized that none of the other planets could sustain life as we know it, either because they are too near the sun and, therefore, too hot, or too far away and much too cold. The one other planet on which speculation suggested that some form of intelligent life might exist has been ruled out. Gerard P. Kuiper, Director of McDonald Observatory, Texas, has said:

> Human life on Mars is entirely out of the question because of the severe night temperature and because there is not enough oxygen.

Indeed, the amount of oxygen is infinitely small, while the night temperature is about -90° F. and only a little above freezing point in daytime, even at the equator.

Can it be that it is all a matter of chance that our planet, among those revolving around the sun, happened to be at the precise climatic distance for the successful production and maintenance of living things? If so, it was a chance that confounds all understanding. Think of all it involves in advantage to ourselves, namely, the scenic glories of hill and vale, seas and lakes, brooks and rivers, forests and wooded glens. Think also of the abundant vegetation, the beauty of the flowers, of seedtime and harvest, and the manifold fruits of the earth; all these are dependent upon a delicate balance of forces and conditions which appear the more miraculous the more we learn about them.

Many relationships existing between the earth and the sun are of vital consequence. The latter is just the right size and the right distance away in order to give and maintain its truly amazing service to our planet. It provides light, power, warmth, and many other blessings, all in serviceable quantities, subject only to terrestrial variations; such as latitude, elevation, proximity to ocean, mountains or desert. It is the power of the sun which provides the winds of the world and these, in turn, carry the rain clouds over the land. Sir John Herschel, the astronomer, suggested what would happen if the sun were suddenly extinguished:

> In three days (72 hours, for there would be no days) — there would, in all probability, not be a vestige of animal or vegetable life on the globe —. The first 48 hours would suffice to precipitate every atom of moisture from the air in deluges of rain and piles of snow, and from that time there would set in a universal frost such as Siberia, or the highest peak in the Himalayas, never felt: a temperature of two and three hundred degrees below zero.

These are some of the more direct calculable effects of the sun's vital contribution to our existence. There are many others, ranging from the beneficial influence which we personally experience, to the mysterious chemical process induced by sunlight which occurs in vegetation. I refer, of course, to what is known as photosynthesis: a process by which a plant is enabled to build up in its chlorophyll cells, carbohydrates from the carbon dioxide in the atmosphere and from the hydrogen of water in the soil.

Animals live on the organic food manufactured by the plants in this way. It follows that all living creatures, either directly or indirectly, not only depend on the sun for light and warmth, but in a miraculous way for all the food they eat. This profound truth was revealed to Moses in words which we can only now begin to understand. He wrote:

> And God said, Behold I have given you every herb bearing seed, which is upon the face of the earth, and every tree, in which is the fruit of a tree yielding seed; and to you it shall be for meat. And to every beast of the earth, and to every fowl of the air, and to everything that creepeth on the earth, wherein there is life, I have given every green herb for meat: and it was so (Genesis 1:29-30).

It may be argued that the Carnivora are flesh-eaters. Even so, were it not for vegetation, both they as well as every other living creature, would quickly die. The diet of the Carnivora comprises sheep, cattle, antelopes and lesser creatures which ultimately are vegetarians, in the main, themselves. The arresting thought is that this truth must have been revealed to Moses at a time when ravenous beasts were proliferating; so much so that at an even earlier date Nimrod became famous as a hunter. Shortly before Moses' death it is recorded in Deuteronomy 7:22, with reference to the advance of the Israelites into Canaan, that:

> The Lord God shall put out those nations before thee little by little, lest the beasts of the field increase upon thee.

Alternatively, the knowledge that no creature preyed upon another until after the Fall, was well known, but first recorded by Moses. It is not possible that any such idea could have been conceived or accepted at a time when beasts and birds of prey abounded, except in one or the other of these two ways.

The Moon

Apart from the reflected light from the sun which the moon sheds upon our planet — adding a rare beauty to the night — it has other functions which have a beneficial influence on the earth. We refer to the ocean tides. These result from the differential gravitational attraction of the moon measured from the near and far sides of the earth, thus giving us high and low tides. Owing to its vastly greater distance away and despite its mass, its differential attraction is much less noticeable as regards the sun, but it is sufficient to cause Spring and Neap tides when these two heavenly bodies are in conjunction or in opposition, respectively.

As with the sun, it is the size and distance of the moon which makes it our good servant, for if the moon were only half its distance away, or if its size were doubled, the rise and fall of the tides would submerge and destroy all harbors in the world as they exist today. Many islands would be covered, together with all coastal plains, and the tidal waves would drive inland for great distances twice every day. The disastrous consequences can barely be imagined.

If the moon were much smaller, or further away, the almost tideless seas would lose their effectiveness in cleansing our harbors. This would apply also to narrow seas and converging coastlines, because a speedier flow of water helps to carry away impurities in heavily populated areas, and, incidentally, improves fishing prospects.

The Earth

When we come to consider our own planet, it is not surprising to find that similar precise conditions are necessary for the initiation and maintenance of its present fruitful condition. It has been estimated that if the earth's diameter were increased by a little over one-sixth, the weight of the atmosphere would be doubled. With twice as much oxygen, scientists tell us, the amount of water would be greatly increased, so that the surface of the planet would be covered with an ocean.

W. J. Humphries, formerly with the United States Weather Bureau, told the American Meteorological Society that if the average temperature of the earth were raised by two or three degrees:

> you could bid good-bye to all the big cities of the earth.

The glaciers and polar ice would melt and that in turn would raise the ocean level by 150 feet. This would inundate hundreds of thousands of square miles of our most fertile lands. Or, if the average mean temperature were only a few degrees colder than now, the great increase in ice and snow in the low latitudes and on the more elevated land would rob the oceans of much of their water. This, again, would result in a greatly decreased rainfall and consequent extension of desert lands, giving a poor prospect for our food supplies. So little, it would seem, is necessary to put fear into the hearts of men, but the delicate balance is preserved by divine decree:

> Who shut up the sea with doors — ? Who, but the great Creator, can say to the oceans: Hitherto shalt thou come, but no further; and here shalt thy proud waves be stayed (Job 38:8, 11).

Adding up these few of the precise conditions concerning the earth, sun and moon, which are found to be necessary for the maintenance of living creatures on our planet, the possibility that all these happy conjunctions happened by mere chance is so remote as to invite immediate rejection. In arriving at this conclusion, we have taken the widest view of the matter. We propose in Part 2 to take a much closer and more restricted viewpoint.

Part II

Instincts

The super-terrestrial evidences of a divine Providence supplying the conditions necessary for our terrestrial existence, cannot be divorced from the idea of Creation. It is certainly beyond the capabilities of our scientists to explain how the sun, moon and earth came to be so intimately and advantageously associated, yet very many are intent on rejecting the Biblical solution of the problem. A super-human Providence is everywhere in evidence and, where this exists, intelligent purpose cannot be denied, nor can initial creation be disallowed.

Super-terrestrial evidence of creation is by no means all the witness thereto that exists. There is far more at hand in terrestrial phenomena: in the fauna and flora which abound on our planet. In this short study we are concentrating on the phenomenon of Instincts more particularly as seen in the behavior of insects. These creatures comprise some of the smallest observable by the naked eye and, therefore, come within the powers of observation of all interested in their examination, without incurring either perils or discomforts.

It is characteristic of instinctive acts that they do not need thought and are never the product thereof. Thought begins when the creature is able, however unconsciously, to hesitate between two or more possibilities, to ponder whether to do or not to do. If you kill an ant near its nest, other ants will flock to their own slaughter in obedience to an instinctive urge, which cannot be varied whatever the circumstances. Initially, the life of an infant child is equally instinctive, but the purpose of its terrestrial existence, unlike that of the ant, is not wholly predetermined, but is shaped by processes of thought as life progresses, and by the varied accumulated thought of many generations. To this we must add the influence of spiritual powers on the mind or soul, but that is another matter.

In its widest connotation, instinct covers reflex actions, such as blinking the eyes in bright light, or automatically straightening the leg when muscles cramp. All such are spontaneous reactions and are neither taught nor acquired. They are of two kinds. The first concerns the preservation of the individual or species. The second, and more important, concerns the purpose of the creature's existence. It is the latter which presents the most powerful argument against the theory of Evolution. Initially, we would say, that chance and purpose are contradictory ideas. A God of chance is a misnomer, and chance, with no God, is another word for chaos.

We can dismiss the first kind with only a brief comment because of its indecisiveness as far as the theory of Evolution is concerned. It does not prove anything to point out the bare fact that a squirrel instinctively climbs a tree when danger threatens, or that a calf, or piglet, turns instinctively to its dam for sustenance. It would be just as impossible to prove that these were very necessary acts, for they were always so, and in the same pattern, as it would be to disprove that they had not been acquired through long and undefined stages.

It is when the creature's reactions are both complex and purposeful that the theory of Evolution proves completely inadequate. No biologist can give a satisfactory explanation, or any explanation at all, of the fine-spun masterpieces of the mindless garden spider; or that of its equally incomprehensible body structure. But the purpose of its web and the need for it to counteract the enormous proliferation of flies and other insect population is very obvious. We might consider another puzzle: how did the spider exist while it invented its truly marvelous and intricate web with the brain it appears never to have possessed? The manufacture of the fiber would suggest another problem. The most reasonable answer is that an intelligence far greater than we can imagine not only conceived the idea, but also provided the instrument for its execution in the humble spider. Writing recently in the *Scientific American* on Spiders' Webs, Peter Wilt stated:

> Every species of spider makes its own kind of web. . . . When a baby spider spins its first web, even if it has never seen a web before, it makes one just like its forebears, but on a smaller scale.

We quote this because it is possible, with patient observation over a period, to confirm the truth of this statement. Yet proof is hardly necessary, for it is impossible to believe that such skill and proficiency could be acquired in the short span of a spider's life.

Expertness of Instinct

Complex and purposeful instincts do not appear as abnormalities or isolated happenings; they are to be found whenever mind, or the ability to think, is lacking. For examples we need only to refer also to the bee and the ant, or to such lesser known marvels as the pronuba moth, or fiddler crab, whose complex behavior is wholly instinctive, as has been proved by experiment. No less automatic is the action of the mindless killer-plants which devour insects. Indeed, the number of living creatures, whose skills are inexplicable by any scientific theory, is beyond enumeration.

It is conceivable that chance might produce one orderly freak which would, apparently, deny its parentage, but when these wonders appear in thousands and in great variety, chance and evolution are impossible explanations.

As indicated, pure instinct occurs where the ability to think is inoperative or non-existent. In fact the two are in inverse ratio. It is as though, where the power of mind does not exist, or is insufficient, God supplied all that is necessary for the perfection of His design in the fulfillment of His purpose. Where there is a complete absence of discernible thought, instinctive acts generally have an intricacy in their execution, and a rigidity in their repetition, which diminish rapidly as the brain, where it exists, begins to function, and, lastly, a perfection in accomplishment which is innate. Compare, for instance, the complex performance of the humble bee from its emergent state, with that of the horse or dog which, having brains, nevertheless, need training if their comparatively useless instincts are to be of service to their master, man. Seemingly, neither the wild horse, nor the Australian dingo, serve any useful purpose in their natural habitat.

The hiatus between the purely instinctive creature and the most intelligent is still more striking. Man, the God-ordained master of every terrestrial creature, is even more helpless at his birth and must be trained in order that he may perform some of the simplest acts of which he is capable. While this is an obvious fact of human life, it is no less true that there appears to be no limit to what he can achieve in the terrestrial sphere and now even far beyond it. The heights and depths of his being, which are barely concealed in childhood, are characterised by an instinctive deviation towards greater or lesser evil as the mind develops, and to transcendent possibilities outside himself when in direct contact with his Creator, through Jesus Christ.

On this point Konrad Lorenz, that great authority on animal behavior, in his recent book *On Aggression* (1965), refers to man's distortion of his own aggressive instincts in the production of weapons for the destruction of his own species and adds:

> If the phrase *Homo sapiens* is not to prove in the end a bad joke, the same energies that drive our animal instincts, must be tapped in a subconscious way, to control them. This can, in theory, be done by consciously setting up the right cultural pressures and values; in time these may become, by natural selection, as ingrained as the marvelous instinctive rituals of the animal world.

Reaction to this conclusion may well be, "What a hopeless prospect." Man cannot create an instinct, nor an abiding selection for his species. He has been trying to do something of the kind from time immemorial and the confusion is plain for all to see. Dr. Lorenz wisely prefaces his suggestion with the words "in theory." We may return to the subject a little later.

The Rigidity of Pure Instinct

The contrast between inherent skills, as observed particularly in insects, and those which are acquired, is in the former's unchangeable nature. If all the means and abilities are provided for the automatic fulfillment of a creature's function in life, then the bestowal of mind is unnecessary. This we judge is true of insects. *For there is nowhere any evidence that instinctive skills are preceded by gradation of inferior skill. Every ant, every bee, every spider fulfills its life purpose with exactitude. There are no bunglers or semi-skilled insects.* A purely instinctive creature cannot transcend its normal behavior. It cannot invent new ways of doing its job.

Unintentionally, perhaps, Divine over-ruling in natural phenomena is suggested by Irson Barnes, late President of the Audubon Society, Washington, D.C., founded to commemorate the great American naturalist of that name. He said:

> Each animal is chained . . . to a distinctive pattern of behavior. . . . Thus a hawk is powerless to alter its tastes or its behavior. This dictate of nature asserts that each form of life shall fulfil its destiny, that no chaos of individual choices shall destroy nature's balance. . . . Each form of life has its essential role in the community.

What Dr. Barnes does not explain, given this fixity of behavior in instinctive creatures, is from whence comes the evident purpose of each. Also, why must we predicate an ordered universe rather than a chaotic one? In human affairs we find much chaos and if "unintelligent" nature reveals a more orderly and purposeful arrangement it can only be because Someone, superhuman, cares about it — Someone with vastly greater intelligence than our own.

Instinct and Feeling

To write about instinct without relating it to feeling might well present an inadequate picture. But in the space available this can only be done, relative to the theory of Evolution, very briefly indeed.

Feeling is of two kinds: physical and emotional. The first has no relevance to our purpose. We are concerned with whether purely instinctive creatures have emotional experiences. A statement by Dr. Timbergen in his *Study of Instincts* (p. 25) has an indirect bearing on this problem. He writes:

> An animal does not react to all the changes in environment which its sense organs receive, but to only a small part of them. This is a basic property of its behavior.

In effect, however, this is a very general statement and is applicable, in measure, to every living creature and even to ourselves. It certainly does not distinguish between purely instinctive creatures (insects) and those endowed with a measure of mind. What the author implies is that instinct knows, or recognizes, only those environments which are either agreeable or hostile. Otherwise, it is truly blind. True instinct can only be a permanent characteristic where mind does not exist, or where it exists, as in infants, it is only until the thinking faculties begin to function. Emotional feeling does not arise as a consequence of a purely instinctive reaction. This has been substantiated by an interesting experiment with an ant taken from a particular nest. In view of the fact that stranger ants from elsewhere found trespassing are attacked and destroyed, this ant was smeared with the juice of a foreign ant and then allowed to return to its own nest. It was very quickly attacked and killed by its own mess-mates because the scent was different. This effect was automatic, and comes within the range of instinctive reactions to hostile environments.

Where there is mind there is also a degree of ability, however slight, to assess the circumstances, or consequences of an event, and it is at this point that emotion is possible. It may be seen in the effect of some deprivation, as when a dog whines because of the absence of its master. This is off-set by tail-wagging and various antics expressing joy at its master's return. Emotional effects of one kind and another are common to many animals, but always in such cases there is some evidence of the working of mind because there is variation in the responses to meet particular cases. For example, you may tease a domestic cat until it seizes your hand or fist with claws and teeth. If you then call its name gently and reprovingly it may then gradually release its hold. This is a common experience. As the compass of the mind increases, so emotional responses become more complex and sometimes more profound and longer lasting. This especially applies to human beings, whose reasonable control over their emotions is not only a very necessary asset, but is also an evidence of their superiority over the beasts.

Emotion would, therefore, appear to be an evidence of the existence of mind and thought, but not necessarily of reasoned thought. If this exercise is the means by which we are to attain perfection, as suggested by Dr. Lorenz, quoted earlier, we are presented with a rather depressing possibility. The only terrestrial creatures to function perfectly within their capabilities are insects, of which no evidence exists that they possess minds. If man could so fashion himself by "right cultural pressures and values" these might, as I understand Dr. Lorenz, result in his "attaining to the marvelous instinctive rituals of the animal world" or, more correctly, of the insect world. So we may conclude from the foregoing that human perfection can be reached when man becomes an automaton, and mind, having fulfilled its purpose, ceases to function.

On a more optimistic note we might consider how far our minds or souls are responsible for our imperfections. We have minds, or centers of control, which are able to misuse or abuse our instincts, or to transcend them. In this sense our minds resemble a form of local government, and this is our privileged endowment. Such acts as self-indulgence, revenge, immorality and the like contradict the essential nature of true instinct, which is to serve an over-all purpose. Does not this suggest a descent from a nobler condition of existence which was then in harmony with our superior gifts?

Part III

Examples

No evidence, in any shape or form, exists as to how insects came by the necessary tools for the accomplishment of their object in life. The existence of these purposes is no less inexplicable, and the fact that they do exist, undeniable. Even a child can understand, in measure, the work done by the humble worm, or the common bee, and yet both the purpose and their specialized equipment defy scientific explanation. We are faced with the same great difficulties when endeavoring to account for the appearance of any other particular creature. We propose, therefore, to consider a few examples.

There are very many creatures whose existence and unique characteristics challenge explanation of the precise kind which is never forthcoming and, in most cases, never attempted. It is possible to feel some sympathy for the hard-baked evolutionist in his endeavors to meet the difficulties which the theory of evolution presents. Unless supported by concrete evidence, such as might be expected from the examination of fossil-bearing strata, even the plea of unlimited time becomes merely a smoke screen to cover up human ignorance where the power of God transcends human understanding. On the other hand, reasonable evidence in support of the Biblical account of how all things came into existence by direct acts of God multiply as we delve into the facts and mysteries of terrestrial life.

Consider first one of our commonest insects, the bee. It is not proposed here to enlarge upon the many marvels involved in the life of this insect, but to confine myself to one matter. In an article by Jean George, which appeared in the *Reader's Digest*, 1966, it is explained how some bees in a hive are nurses whose task is to feed the queen bee and the larvae. The milk for this purpose is formed by special glands in the nurse bee's head. Other bees are provided with a different kind of chemical laboratory which turns honey into beeswax. These chemical factories are unfailing. It is not magic which enables some workers to provide "bee-milk" and others "beeswax." The secret is hidden in the infinitesimal genes of the bee. If we could possibly allow that a lucky chance enabled the bee to evolve along a particular line in order to produce honey, it remains quite impossible for the evolutionist to explain the purposeful co-ordination in the production of bee-milk and beeswax from the same type of insect, or the maintenance of a correct proportion of each type. The failure of either would upset the whole colony and quickly lead to its extinction, but the productions do not fail – and that is a miracle. The overall evidence of design and balance in nature is one of the strongest arguments in favor of Creation by God.

The Butterfly

Another common insect is the butterfly. Its tongue is as long as its body. Butterflies live on nectar which is concealed in deep pockets of flowers. To reach their necessary food they must unroll their tongues and thrust them far down into these recesses. It is quite useless to pretend that these tongues which are, in fact, sucking tubes have developed over long ages to meet an urgent need. The question immediately arises as to how those insects could possibly have survived during the very long period in which the supposed development was taking place. We are faced with another pertinent question: If the butterflies could live through even a thousand butterfly generations during the development period, why need they bother to develop so delicate an instrument? If this was really true, one could only exclaim, what persistence! what determination! what foresight! for an end so deeply concealed in the heart of a flower!

The same argument can be applied to the elephant's trunk. If it was not a part of the original animal eating and drinking must still have been possible without the trunk, and, therefore, why develop this awkward appendage? The answer surely is that the animal always had a trunk. There is no such animal existing with half a trunk, and fossil evidence is completely lacking of such a freak.

Fishes that Fish

The following is a quote from a pamphlet entitled *Partnership: Planned or Accidental?* by T. W. Carron:

> Walking by the seashore recently, I watched an angler casting his line into the sea. It set up a train of thought. The fish he eventually caught fell a victim to the man's pre-arranging and interconnecting intelligence. The poor fish could not know that the tasty morsel he saw hid a fatal hook by which it would be hauled up out of its native element to provide a meal for the fisherman. Then I recalled that there are fish, which themselves fish with rod and line, so that thus man was not the first angler. There are, in fact, a number of species of Angling fishes. The Oceanic Anglerfish (Gigantactus macronema) has a line four times the length of its body with an enticing "bait" at the end. Some species actually have a rod. Lasiognathus has one, and the line extends beyond the "bait" ending in a triangle of hooks. This fish's mouth is peculiarly contrived, too, to deal with the catch. The Sea Devils, another group of Angler fish, live in the middle of the depths of the ocean where there is little or no light. In these the female fish, moving about in the darkness, depend upon a luminous lure. The males of this group are smaller — mere hangers-on — attached to the female, sometimes literally. Here then is the "compleat angler." Was it its own intelligence which taught the Angler fish to catch its fellow denizens of the deep? Did it, before it became an angler, think up the complex idea of growing a rod and line with a "bait" and hooks on the end, and then begin to grow these appendages? Obviously nonsense! But is the Darwinian "explanation" any more sensible? Could chance variations even over millions of years, "guided" by Natural Selection and the struggle to survive, produce a complicated mechanism like this? In a word, did the Angler fishes evolve, or were they created? I'm asking you.

The Moth and the Yucca Plant

The Yucca plant grows in the desert and has an attractive flower. The circumstances of its survival would suggest that it was a hardy plant, while the white lily-like flowers, protected by clusters of sharp sword-like leaves, might suggest that the plant was rejoicing in its independence. But this is far from the truth. Its very existence depends upon the activities of a tiny white moth, called

Pronuba. During the day this pronuba moth hides underground. When night comes it shows itself and flaps around but never eats anything. The Yucca buds open at nightfall and bursts into flower and on certain nights give forth a strong fragrance. It is at this precise moment that the Pronuba moth comes forth from its cocoon beneath the sand and, attracted by the scent from the flowers, flies to its only supply of food — the seeds of the Yucca plant. It goes to the top of the stamens of the nearest flower and scrapes together a wad of pollen and, carrying a big load in its jaws and tentacles, flies to another Yucca plant. It goes backward to the bottom of the flower, pierces a hole with its egg-laying needle, and lays its eggs among the seed cells at the base of the pistil where there is a cavity just the right size to take the load of pollen. The moth stuffs this in and pads it in so as to ensure that the pollen tubes will do their job and fertilize the seeds where it has laid its eggs. The mother moth has thus "planned" ahead and "deliberately" bred the plants so that her offspring will have a supply of food where they are born. The eggs are ready to hatch when the seeds are about ripe, so when the larvae (caterpillars) emerge they have an ample supply of delicious food at hand. They eat their fill of seeds, grow and cut a hole in the pod, lowering themselves to the ground by spinning a silken thread. The mother moth never eats — all she does is lay eggs, pollinate the Yucca plant and then die. A remarkable part of the whole business is that the babies eat only about a fifth of the seeds in the pod, which allows the rest of the seeds to mature and the plant to continue.

The explanation of this mysterious partnership is anyone's guess. Until someone can account for the whole process it would be foolish to deny that it is an evidence of God's own handiwork. The catalog of nature's wonders could be extended to hundreds of examples which mock the theory of Evolution and glorify the Creator. So we return to the words of Paul:

> The invisible things of Him from the creation of the world are clearly seen, being understood by the things that are made, even His eternal power and Godhead.

SAN JOSE CHRISTIAN SCHOOL